The Learning Works

VICTORY
The Challenge of International Sports

Written by Diane Sylvester and Karen Dick
Illustrated by Beverly Armstrong
Ages 9 and Up

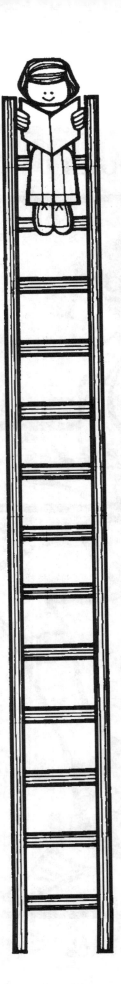

The Learning Works

Cover Design & Illustration:
Bev Armstrong

Editing and Typography:
Kimberley A. Clark

Copyright © 1996
The Learning Works, Inc.
P.O. Box 6187
Santa Barbara, California 93160

ISBN: 0-88160-271-X

Contents

Introduction

Victory is the goal of all Olympic athletes. It is the reason for their struggle and the reward for their effort. This book, entitled **Victory**, is about these athletes and their games. It is a collection of information and activities for use at home or school. It contains information about the Olympic Games, both ancient and modern, and many activities to extend understanding of the Olympic tradition and to encourage creative thinking. The pages in this book provide experiences in such curricular areas as history, humanities, language arts, math, research skills, science, social studies, and creative problem solving. They may be used together, as a cohesive study unit, or separately, to supplement other home or classroom learning experiences.

The ancient Olympic Games in Greece were not only a demonstration of athletic excellence, but also an opportunity to develop the attitudes of sportsmanship and ethical conduct. The goals of the modern Olympics reflect these ancient traditions. The aims of the Olympic movement are to encourage the physical and moral qualities that are the basis of sport, to promote world peace by bringing young people together, and to spread the Olympic principles as a means of establishing good will.

The ideas and traditions of the Olympic Games provide a perfect framework for becoming aware of the differences in human experience, considering current economic and political issues, appraising shared values, and setting individual goals. The activities in this book may be used as written assignments or as the basis for thought-provoking discussions on these or other related topics.

Name _____

A Glance at the Past

The barefoot runners were tense as they waited for the trumpeters to signal the start of the race. Their oiled bodies glistened in the warm Grecian sun. They believed that victory was a way of honoring the gods and earning immortality for themselves and fame for the cities they represented. The winner of this important race, held in 776 B.C., was Coroebus, a runner from the city of Elis. At the celebration that followed his victory, he was wrapped in a purple cloak and presented with a crimson apple.

Ancient Greece was not a centrally governed country. Rather, it was a loose collection of separately governed city-states—neighboring cities which had grown so large and powerful that they functioned politically more like sovereign states or small countries than like cities within a country. The people of ancient Greece valued excellence and admired aesthetic, intellectual, and athletic achievement. Rivalries grew up among these cities, and representatives from them competed vigorously on both the athletic field and the battlefield.

The ancient Greeks chose Olympia as one site for their athletic contests. Later, the events held there became known as the Olympic Games. Olympia was a plain in Elis. On it, the Greeks built temples to Zeus, ruler of the gods and of heaven, and to Hera, his wife. Like a magnet, these temples attracted religious pilgrims from near and far. At first, the plain was the site of worship services and of religious celebrations. Later, games and other athletic contests were added to what became known as the Olympic Festival, and a stadium was built.

The Greek **stadium** was *not* a large, tiered structure of benches or seats surrounding an athletic playing field. Instead, it was a track approximately 607 feet long, built for the running of footraces. In fact, the word *stadion* came to be used as the chief Greek unit of measure for distances.

Name _____

A Glance at the Past
(continued)

During the first fifty-two years of the Olympic Games, a sprint over the full length of the stadium was the only event. Then, a footrace two *stadia* long was run in the XIVth Olympiad. Later, wrestling matches, chariot races, and other contests were added.

Before the ancient games began, the athletes, trainers, referees, judges, and trumpeters paraded to Olympia. On the day of the games, the athletes registered and took part in purification rites and in ceremonial bathing, during which they swore to observe all rules and to uphold the high ideals of sportsmanship. Among the crowd gathered at Olympia to see the games were poets, philosophers, politicians, soldiers, peddlers, dancers, gamblers, acrobats, and clowns, but no women. Women were not allowed to participate in the events—or even to watch them!

By our standards, the accommodations for the thousands of visitors who journeyed to Olympia for the festival were spartan indeed. There were no hotels and few tents. Most spectators slept on the ground in the open. Drinking water was available at only nine sources, and bathing facilities were scarce. By the middle of the fourth century B.C., the Olympic facilities had been improved somewhat. The leonidaeum had been built to house important spectators, and a gymnasium had been constructed for the competing athletes.

For nearly twelve centuries after Coroebus's victory, the Olympic Games were held in Greece every four years without interruption. Not even wars were allowed to interfere with this schedule. During the month of the Olympic Festival, a truce was declared between all warring city-states. Then, in A.D. 394, Emperor Theodosius the Great of Rome gave orders to halt the games, which had degenerated since the Roman invasion of Greece. The glorious tradition of the ancient Olympic Games was at an end.

Activities

1. Jim Thorpe, Carl Lewis, and Jackie Joyner-Kersee are famous American track and field athletes who performed well in past Olympic Games. Imagine that Jim, Carl, and Jackie are sitting in a stadium having a conversation with Coroebus about the Olympics. Write down in dialogue form the questions they might ask and the replies that might be given. Include at least one question and reply for each athlete.

2. Pretend that you are a victorious sprinter in an ancient Olympic contest. Create a story, play, poem, or song about the race, the people who came to cheer for you, and the excitement of being a champion.

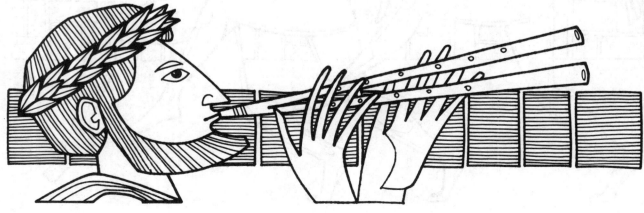

Name _____

Athletes From Long Ago

In ancient Greece, athletes were selected to participate in the Olympic Games at elimination trials that were held in various parts of the country. The outstanding performers came to Olympia, where they trained intensively for ten months. They lived in gymnasiums and worked with their trainers every day.

A winning athlete's only official reward was a crown of olive leaves cut from a sacred olive tree, but statues and other works of art were often created to honor Olympic heroes. A victorious athlete had tremendous prestige in his hometown. If he had been truly outstanding, a portion of the city wall was knocked down for him to enter upon his return. This gesture symbolized that the citizens of the city had great faith in his abilities and believed that he would be able to protect them from enemy attack.

Coroebus became famous because he won the first recorded Olympic race; however, many historians are convinced that the greatest star of the ancient Olympic Games was Milo of Croton. Milo, who lived during the sixth century B.C., won the wrestling crown six times. For hundreds of years after his victories, people still sang and wrote of his amazing feats. It was said that Milo developed his astounding strength by carrying a calf on his shoulders until it was a full-grown bull. According to one account, Milo challenged all onlookers to push him off an oiled discus, but no one could. To impress his admirers, Milo would tie a cord around his forehead and hold his breath until the veins in his head swelled enough to break the cord.

Fame also came to Polydamas of Thessaly. Polydamas was champion of an event called the **pancratium**. The name of this event is derived from the Greek word *pankrates*, meaning "all-powerful." The original intent of the pancratium was to prepare men for battle. It was an athletic contest involving both boxing and wrestling skills. In hand-to-hand combat, contestants tried to knock each other over by punching, wrestling, or kicking. When one man went down, his opponent jumped on him and kicked, hit, or even tried to strangle him. Only biting and eye gouging were not allowed. When one contestant had been rendered unconscious or signaled defeat, the other contestant was declared the winner. Polydamas is said to have killed a lion with his bare hands and to have stopped a moving chariot by seizing the back with one hand.

Another ancient pancratium hero was Arrachion of Phigalia, who was awarded the victory after he died in the stadium. His opponent raised his hand in defeat without realizing that Arrachion was dead.

Name _____

Athletes From Long Ago
Activity Sheet

Choose an *ancient* Olympic hero to be the star of a *modern* television commercial.

1. What product will the athlete endorse? _____

   Why? _____

   _____

   _____

2. Think of a catchy slogan or jingle that might be used to promote this product. Write it here.

   _____

   _____

   _____

   _____

3. Of all the places in the world, what setting would you use to film the commercial? Identify or describe it here.

   _____

   _____

4. On the lines below, write a short commercial script for the athlete to read. If you need additional space, use a separate sheet of paper.

   _____

   _____

   _____

   _____

   _____

   _____

   _____

   _____

Name _____

The End and the Beginning

With the rise of the Roman Empire, the entire atmosphere of the Greek Olympic Games changed. The games gradually lost their religious significance and became more like a carnival. The athletes began demanding money for their efforts, and profit became the incentive for participation. As financial rewards became greater and greater, corruption set in. It was because of this corruption that the Roman Emperor Theodosius banned the games in A.D. 394. After nearly 1,170 years of continual competition, the Olympic flame was extinguished.

The idea of reviving the games was born in the 1880s, when Olympia was excavated. Among those who wandered through its ruins was a French nobleman named Baron Pierre de Coubertin. He had been commissioned by the French government to study physical education. He became more and more convinced that a revival of the games would improve overall physical fitness and encourage international understanding. He envisioned athletes coming from all over the world to share athletic fields, meals, and shelter. He felt that mutual respect would be the natural product of their firsthand knowledge of one another's customs and cultures.

At last, Pierre de Coubertin's dream came true. After much hard work, the first modern Olympic Games were held in 1896 in Athens, Greece. Thirteen countries participated with athletes from ten of them winning medals. The winning countries were Australia, Austria, Denmark, England, France, Germany, Greece, Hungary, Switzerland, and the United States. There were only nine events in 1896: cycling, fencing, gymnastics, shooting, swimming, tennis, track and field, weight lifting, and wrestling. To emphasize his high ideals, de Coubertin created an Olympic charter and oath and instituted the opening and closing ceremonies.

Although the modern Olympic Games have not noticeably advanced the cause of peace, they have promoted the high ideals of sportsmanship, friendly competition, and human achievement. Only through the hard work and perseverance of Baron de Coubertin was it possible for the extinguished Olympic flame to be rekindled.

Activity

Summer Olympic Sites

Athens (1896)
Paris (1900, 1924)
St. Louis (1904)
London (1908, 1948)
Stockholm (1912)
Antwerp (1920)
Amsterdam (1928)
Los Angeles (1932, 1984)
Berlin (1936)
Helsinki (1952)

Melbourne (1956)
Rome (1960)
Tokyo (1964)
Mexico City (1968)
Munich (1972)
Montreal (1976)
Moscow (1980)
Seoul (1988)
Barcelona (1992)
Atlanta (1996)

Locate these cities on a globe or map, and then decide which Olympic city you would like to visit. What factors influenced your decision? Make a poster that includes drawings of five attractions that distinguish or characterize the city.

Name _____

Winning an Olympic Bid

The host city of the Olympic Games has a major responsibility to prepare facilities for the athletes and the competitions. The host city must organize and oversee the ceremonies as well as the athletic and cultural events. For the 1996 Olympic Games, Athens, Greece; Belgrade, Yugoslavia; Manchester, England; Melbourne, Australia; Toronto, Canada; and Atlanta, Georgia in the United States sought this challenge. The International Olympic Committee (IOC) selected Atlanta, Georgia. The dream of being an Olympic City did not happen overnight. The hard work began in 1987 when city leaders and officials faced the task of convincing the United States Olympic Committee and then the International Olympic Committee that their city should have the bid. The Atlanta Committee for the Olympic Games promoted their city as having superior air travel and telecommunications, world class hotels and hospitality, modern sports facilities, and a friendly, multicultural community.

Activities

1. Of all the remaining cities in the world, which one would you select as the site for future Olympic Games? Defend your choice by making a list of your reasons for it.

2. Form small committees that will each represent a city that hasn't yet been chosen as an Olympic site. Each committee is responsible for developing a plan to convince the IOC that its city should be the choice for the next Olympic Games. Present the findings to the class. Analyze the presentations and then reach a consensus on which city should be chosen.

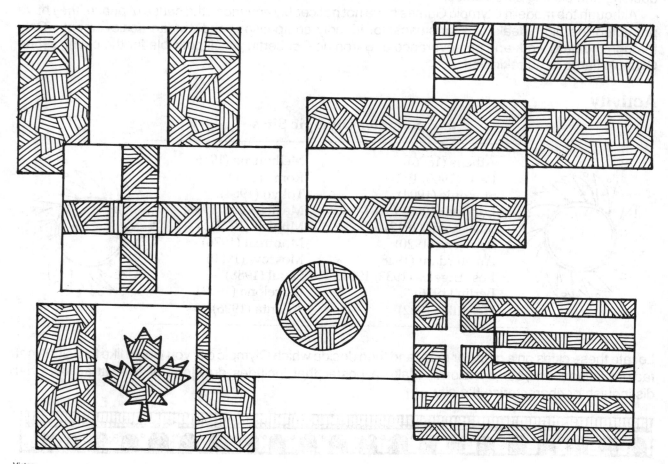

Name _____

It's Greek to Me

The English words listed below are derived from Greek. Be a word detective. Use a dictionary to discover the derivation of each word. Then choose your favorite word and write a short story about how that word came to be used as it is. You might explain why the word was needed or tell about the circumstances under which it was first used. Base your story on facts, but use your imagination to fill in the missing details.

1. athlete
2. decathlon
3. gymnasium
4. hippodrome
5. marathon

6. Olympiad
7. pentathlon
8. promethean
9. spartan
10. stadium

Cipher is a method of systematically changing a written text to conceal its meaning by substituting new letters for existing ones. See if you can decipher the following message written by Baron de Coubertin.

D J P   T U W D   R T F U E D N G D   D J R G Q   R G

___ ___ ___   ___ ___ ___ ___   ___ ___ ___ ___ ___ ___ ___ ___ ___   ___ ___ ___ ___ ___   ___ ___

D J P   U H Z T F R O   Q N T P W   R W   G U D

___ ___ ___   ___ ___ ___ ___ ___ ___ ___   ___ ___ ___ ___ ___   ___ ___   ___ ___ ___

D U   Y R G   M X D   D U   D N S P   F N E D.

___ ___   ___ ___ ___   ___ ___ ___   ___ ___   ___ ___ ___ ___   ___ ___ ___ ___.

Hint: Look for small words and double letters. Notice how frequently certain letters are used and where letter groups are repeated.

Activities

1. Some Olympic events involve running. The word **run** is a part of many terms and expressions that are used both in and out of sports. Make a list of these expressions. For example, you might begin with the baseball term **home run**.

2. Learn how to say "hello" and to count from one to ten in at least one other language.

3. Make a list of twenty words that are related in some way to the Olympics. These words might be names of athletes, items of equipment, actual events, or specific locations. On a separate sheet of paper, write each word in scrambled form. Then give the scrambled version to a friend to unscramble.

4. Use the ten words listed at the top of this page in a story about the ancient or the modern Olympic Games.

Name _____

Clues to the Past

Official written records were not kept during the early days of the ancient Olympic Games. However, toward the end of the fifth century B.C., Hippios of Elis, a philosopher, published a list of Olympic victors, which Aristotle revised and updated a century later. Even though neither one of these lists survived to our time, other writers referred to them in their works making it possible to compile a fairly complete catalog of ancient winners.

As interesting as these lists may be, they provide only an incomplete history of the Olympic Games. To learn more about this eventful period, historians and archaeologists have turned to other sources. Some of these sources include archaeological ruins and artifacts, monuments, murals, words spoken in Greek dramas, paintings on fine pottery, and odes.

One of the finest sources of pictorial information about the Olympics is Athenian pottery. This pottery includes not only magnificent vases, cups, and bowls, but also **amphorae**. Amphorae were special jars with large, oval bodies; narrow, cylindrical necks; and two gracefully curved handles. They were commissioned by city-states to honor their athletic heroes. Once finished, they were filled with olive oil collected from sacred olive trees and awarded to the victors of sporting events. Scenes painted on this pottery depict pole vaulters, discus throwers, boxers, and trainers caring for athletes.

Ancient Greek artists and sculptors often ignored anatomical accuracy to create designs that were symmetrical and balanced, designs that they found aesthetically pleasing. Modern athletes who have tried to assume the positions illustrated on ancient Greek pottery have found the task to be difficult, if not impossible.

Grecian odes, rich in imagery, were commissioned by the wealthiest victors and were sung at their victory celebrations. Many of them were written by Pindar, a Greek lyric poet who lived and wrote between 522 and 443 B.C. Among his works are forty-four odes celebrating victories in national games. Complex in content and of varied meter and length, these odes are of such high quality that they can be enjoyed today for their poetic as well as their historic value.

The arts, now a valuable source of information about the ancient Olympics, have long been associated with these games. The Greeks admired both artistic and athletic achievement. A festival of the arts became a part of the ancient Olympic Games in the eighth century B.C. and has been a part of every modern Olympics.

Name _____

Clues to the Past
Activity Sheet

1. First, choose a contender for the next Olympics. Then, draw a rough sketch or silhouette of this athlete taking part in his or her event. Try to imitate the classic lines and stylized form of the drawings on ancient Greek pottery. Finally, transfer your design to the Greek vase outlined below.

2. Fine arts were added to the modern Olympics in 1912. Among the events included were architecture, literature, music, painting, and sculpture. Organize a Fine Arts Competition with some of your friends or classmates. Decide on the events you will include, invite other "artists" to participate, and set a date for the display of finished projects.

3. Create an Olympic montage using pictures from old magazines and newspapers. Emphasize one event or some particular aspect of the games.

4. Read John Keats's "Ode on a Grecian Urn" or Allen Tate's "Ode to the Confederate Dead." Experiment with writing a serious ode in praise of someone or something of importance.

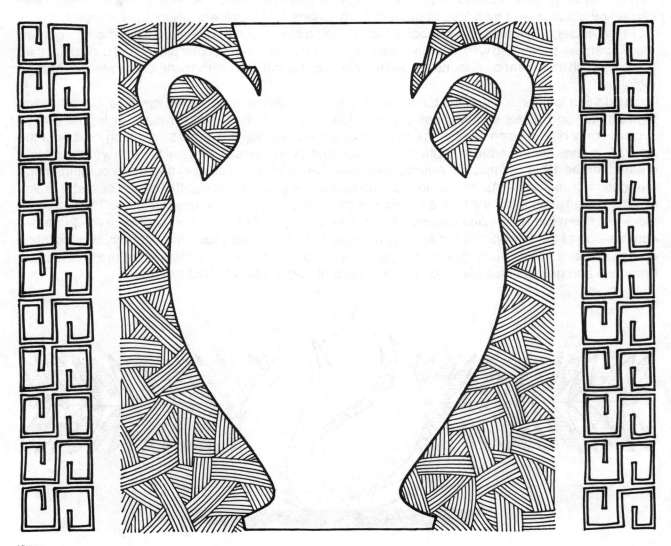

Name _____

Olympic Symbolism

As the trumpets blare and the parade of brightly dressed athletes begins, thousands of spectators have the opportunity to participate in the traditions that have long been a part of the Olympic Games. They cheer as the Olympic flag is raised. This flag was first flown in public at Alexandria, Greece, in 1914 and first waved over an Olympic competition in 1920 at Antwerp, Belgium. It is a borderless white banner that bears the official Olympic symbol, five interlocking rings. These rings stand for the five participating continents—Europe, Asia, Africa, Australia, and America (North, Central, and South)—and symbolize the athletic brotherhood of the planet earth. The blue, yellow, black, green, and red rings incorporate at least one color from every national flag.

Finally, the most exciting moment of the ceremonies arrives. A runner carrying the Olympic torch enters the stadium, climbs the stairs, and lights the Olympic flame. This flame will burn continuously throughout the games. It has traveled a long way to be here. At the original site of the ancient Olympic Games in Olympia, Greece, this symbolic flame was lit from the light of the sun and then carried into the stadium, where it was handed to a priestly "king" of the new Olympiad. He passed the torch to the leader of a team of runners, who carried it to a nearby grove of trees dedicated to the father of the modern Olympics, Baron Pierre de Coubertin. There it was used to light an altar flame that would burn throughout the games. From Olympia it was taken by young athletes to Athens, Greece. Then, it was carried by airplane and by relays of runners from Athens to the present site of the Olympics.

In the ancient Olympics, the symbol of victory was a crown of olive leaves. In the modern games, the winners are presented with medals—gold for first place, silver for second place, and bronze for third place—which they wear on ribbons around their necks. Fourth-, fifth-, and sixth-place winners receive diplomas.

In addition to the rings and the torch, which are perpetual symbols of the Olympics, cities hosting the summer and winter competitions are permitted to design their own symbols, or logos. These symbols may be representative of the cities or countries in which the games are being held or of the spirit the games are intended to capture and encourage. The Atlanta Centennial Torch was the design created for the 1996 Olympics in Atlanta, Georgia. The torch is the spirit of the future burning on the foundation of the past. As the flame reaches upward, it gradually takes the shape of a star which symbolizes an athlete striving for the excellence that makes Olympic competition great. The emerging stars represent the hopes and dreams of world-wide unity and peace. The handle of the torch is a combination of the Olympic Rings and the number 100 which recognizes the centennial celebration of the Olympics. The colors, green and gold, were chosen because they represent the green laurel branches and gold medals given to victors in ancient and modern Olympic Games.

Name _____

Olympic Symbolism
Activity Sheet

1. In the year A.D. 3000, when the first inter-planetary Olympic Games are held, a new Olympic symbol will be needed.

   In the rectangle provided, create a design that symbolizes galaxy-wide participation in these games.

2. Traditions help to make events memorable. On the lines below, describe a tradition which you would like to initiate and see repeated that would be associated with an athletic event or some other special occasion.

_____

_____

_____

_____

_____

_____

_____

_____

_____

3. The motto for the Olympic Games is *Citius, Altius, Fortius*. Translated from Latin, it means "Swifter, Higher, Stronger." On the line below, write a motto for yourself, your family, or your school in which you catch a particular spirit or express a specific goal in a few well-chosen words.

_____

CITIUS · ALTIUS · FORTIUS

Name _____

Olympic Pageantry

Opening Ceremony

A special ceremony marks the opening of the Olympic Games. This ceremony begins with the Parade of Nations—one of the most colorful parades in the world. It consists of athletes from each of the participating countries, dressed in beautiful national costumes, designer fashions, or color-coordinated sportswear. Because Greece is the country in which the Olympic Games originated many centuries ago, Greek athletes are always given the honor of leading the parade. Athletes from other nations march in alphabetical order by country, according to the language of the host country. In 1952, the United States athletes marched next to last because Finland was the host country, and United States is spelled *Yhdysvallat* in Finnish. In Barcelona, they entered early in the parade because the United States is spelled *Estados Unidos* in Spanish. Athletes from the host nation always march last.

As the final delegation passes the reviewing stand, the head of the host nation and the president of the International Olympic Committee proclaim that the games are officially open. The Olympic flag is slowly raised while a band plays the Olympic hymn. The political head of the city in which the games are being held is presented with an official Olympic flag, which will fly over the city hall until the next Olympics.

And now, the moment for which the audience has been eagerly waiting arrives. A runner carrying the Olympic torch enters the stadium. The runner circles the field and then climbs the stairs to light the flame that will burn throughout the games. Together, the athletes take an oath to uphold the highest traditions of Olympic competition. Finally, hundreds of doves are released to symbolize the spirit of the games—the shared desire for victory and for peace.

Winner's Ceremony

Another special ceremony is held for the winners of each event. Medals on ribbons are placed around the necks of the competitors who have placed first, second, and third. These medal recipients stand on a raised platform, with the first-place winner between and slightly higher than the other two. The other athletes and the spectators stand at attention while the flag of the winner's country is raised on a central pole and the band plays that country's national anthem.

Olympic Pageantry
(continued)

Closing Ceremony

The closing ceremony is simpler than the opening one. The athletes do not parade by nation. They enter the stadium in no particular order to symbolize the unity and friendship of the Olympic Games. Only six athletes from each country are allowed to participate. The flag bearers of each nation form a semicircle. First, the Greek national anthem is played, and the Greek flag is raised. Next, the flag of the host country is raised, and then, the flag of the nation selected to host the next Olympic Games is raised. Finally, the Olympic flame is solemnly extinguished. While the Olympic flag is being lowered, the Olympic hymn is played one final time. With the official ceremony over, the host city presents an entertainment extravaganza.

Activities

1. Look at a globe or map of the world. Plan a route that runners carrying the Olympic flame could take from Olympia, in Greece, to your hometown. Pay close attention to geographic barriers, such as mountain ranges, rivers, and oceans.

2. In German, United States is spelled *Vereinigten Staaten*. Find out the spelling of United States in French and Italian.

3. The prize for the first-place winner in the ancient games was a crown of olive leaves. The prize for the first-place winner in the modern games is a silver gilt medal containing at least six grams of fine gold. (The games in Paris in 1900 remain the only Olympics where valuable pieces of art were awarded instead of medals.) In the space below, draw or describe the first-place prize for the 2196 Olympic Games.

Name _____

Victorious Vocabulary

Test your knowledge of Olympic sports vocabulary. Each of the terms listed in the left-hand column is associated with an Olympic sport listed in the right-hand column. Match the terms with the sports by writing the correct letter on each line. If you need help, look up the terms that puzzle you in a dictionary.

_____	1. high-sticking	A. archery
_____	2. bull's eye	B. boxing
_____	3. butterfly	C. equestrian events
_____	4. schussing	D. fencing
_____	5. jab	E. figure skating
_____	6. camel	F. gymnastics
_____	7. sculls	G. hockey
_____	8. take down	H. judo
_____	9. pigeon	I. rowing
_____	10. long horse	J. shooting
_____	11. parry	K. skiing
_____	12. piaffe	L. swimming
_____	13. black belt	M. weight lifting
_____	14. clean and jerk	N. wrestling

Activities

1. Make a list of all of the words you can think of that relate to the idea of winning. For example, you might start with **conquer**.

2. Words in the form of slogans or mottoes are used to influence people. A slogan should be short, have rhythm, make you stop and think, and perhaps, use words in an unusual or clever way. Write a slogan about athletics, the Olympics, or sportsmanship.

3. Design a poster based on the slogan you wrote in activity 2.

OOOOO WHO GETS THE PRIZE? OOOOO
THE ONE WHO TRIES!

Name _____

Design Time

1. The design for the Olympic medal was created in 1928 by Italian artist Giuseppe Cassioli. Since 1972, Cassioli's design has been used on the front of the medal, and the host city's design is used on the back of the medal. In the space below, create a design for the back side which would be appropriate for the next Olympic Games, either summer or winter.

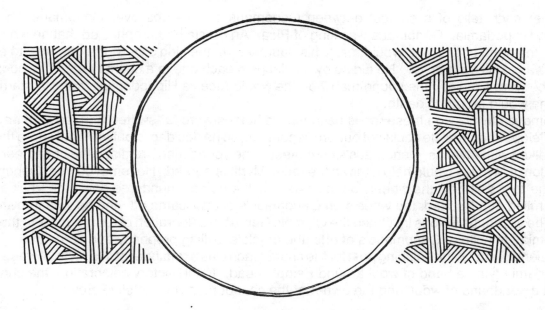

2. On a separate sheet of paper, design a postage stamp to commemorate the Olympics.

3. Pretend that the 2008 Olympics will be held in your hometown. Think about what you would like to have people remember about your town. Then, design a special symbol for these games which expresses both the spirit of the Olympics and the special atmosphere of the place in which you live.

4. Design a T-shirt for the Olympics of 2020 or for one of the Olympics of the past.

5. Misha the Bear was the official mascot for the 1980 Olympic Games held in Moscow. Sam the Olympic Eagle was the official mascot of the 1984 Olympics in Los Angeles. The mascot for the 1996 Games mascot is *Izzy,* a futuristic, computer-generated character with large, starry eyes and oversized sneakers. Izzy is able to morph into all sizes and shapes to become a participant in all Olympic activities. On a separate sheet of paper, create an official mascot for one of the Olympic competitions of the past.

Olympic Myths

Myths about the origins of the Olympic Games are varied, but all of them have something to do with a fierce contest. One myth tells of a terrible feud between Zeus and Cronos, the two most powerful Greek gods. According to this account, they battled on Mount Olympus for possession of the earth. Zeus won, and athletic contests have been held near this site ever since.

Another myth tells of a contest between Oenomaus and Pelops over Oenomaus's beautiful daughter, Hippodamia. Oenomaus was king of Pisa. An oracle had prophesied that he would lose his life at the hand of one who would marry his daughter. In the king's view, the only way to escape this fate was to kill each suitor. He did so by challenging each one to a chariot race. The conditions of the race were simple: if the young man won, he would receive Hippodamia's hand in marriage; if he lost, he would be put to death.

Oenomaus always won these races because his horses were far swifter than those of any other mortal. Pelops knew that he could not outrun Oenomaus, so he decided to outwit him. Before the race, Pelops talked with Myrtilus, Oenomaus's charioteer. The young man promised the charioteer half of the kingdom if Myrtilus would help him win the race. Myrtilus agreed. He removed from Oenomaus's chariot the pins that held the wheels on the axle. As the horses thundered down the track and the chariots rolled at full speed, the wheels on Oenomaus's chariot came off, and he was thrown to his death. The victorious Pelops instituted the Olympic Games in celebration of his marriage to the lovely Hippodamia. In spite of Oenomaus's efforts, the oracle's chilling prophecy had come true.

In ancient Olympia, the finishing post for the chariot race was a reminder of this myth. It was a statue of Hippodamia tying a band of wool around Pelop's head. In the victory celebration, the charioteer received a headband of wool, and the owner of the chariot received the olive crown.

The Greek strong man Heracles plays an important role in several myths about the Olympics. Pindar, the Greek poet, attributed the beginning of the Olympic Games to Heracles's victory over King Augeas of Elis. In addition, Heracles is supposed to have established the length of the stadium by pacing off six hundred steps. Another myth tells that the length of the stadium was set at six hundred feet because that was the distance the amazing Heracles could run on one lungful of air.

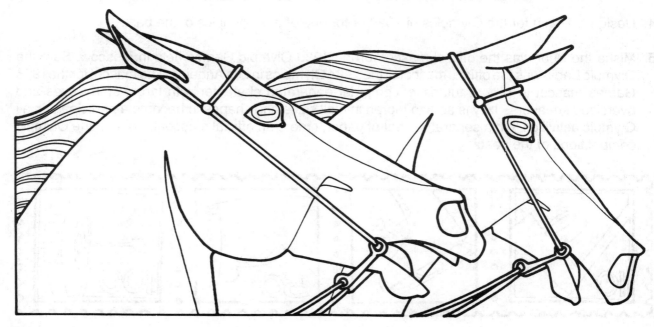

Olympic Myths
Activity Sheet

1. Augeas, the king of Elis, had three thousand oxen, whose stalls had not been cleaned in thirty years. First, read about how Eurystheus commanded Heracles to clean these stalls in one day and about how Heracles diverted a river to do the job. Then, invent an original game or event for the Olympics that future scholars might interpret as being based on this myth.

   Name of game or event: _____

   Brief description: _____

   _____

   _____

   _____

2. Olympus is actually a mountain range in northern Greece which separates Macedonia from Thessaly. It is twenty-five miles long and rises to a height of 9,570 feet. Its summit is the highest point in Greece and is perpetually covered with snow and frequently hidden by clouds. It was here, according to Greek myth, that the twelve most important gods and goddesses—known as the Olympians—lived. Look up the names of the twelve Olympians, and inscribe them on the stone below.

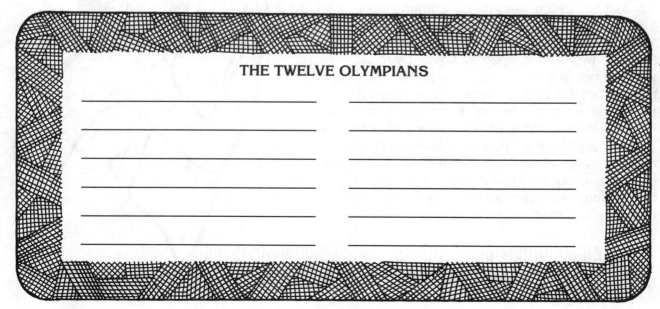

THE TWELVE OLYMPIANS

Name _____

Women in the Olympics

When crowds gathered at Olympia to watch the games, among them were rich people and poor, young people and old, but no women. Women were not allowed to participate in the ancient Olympic Games or even to watch them. If a woman was found at the games, she was immediately taken to a cliff overlooking the Alpheus River and thrown off.

One brave woman, Callipatira of Rhodes, was willing to risk death to watch her son participate in an Olympic boxing match. To avoid detection, she cleverly disguised herself as a trainer and entered the stadium wearing a long cloak. When her son won his match, she became so excited that she leaped over a barricade and rushed out to embrace him. Unfortunately, as she did so, her cloak flew open, and the other spectators were shocked to discover that a woman was in their midst. Callipatira was luckier than other women guilty of the same offense because her father and her brother had been Olympic champions. In their honor, her life was spared; but it was decreed that all trainers and athletes would appear in the stadium without clothing to prevent similar deceptions in the future.

There was one Olympic event, chariot racing, which women were allowed to enter—if they owned the chariot team, trained it themselves, and hired a driver, or charioteer—but they were not even allowed to watch the race. Cynisca, daughter of the King of Sparta, was an expert horse breeder and trainer. Twice her teams won the chariot championship.

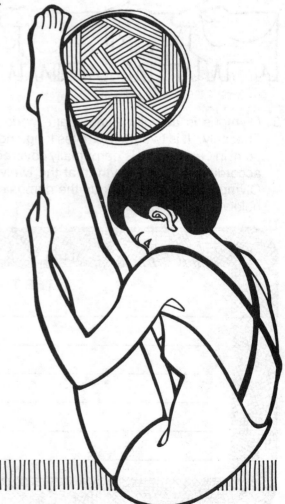

As early as the sixth century B.C., Greek women began holding games of their own. These games, called the **Heraea** in honor of the goddess Hera, took place quadrennially in off-Olympic years. There were fewer events in the Heraea than in the Olympics. Among the Heraean events were footraces. Participants raced in tunics, and the winners were crowned with olive wreaths.

When the Olympic tradition was revived in 1896, Baron Pierre de Coubertin stated that allowing women to compete in them would be "against the laws of nature." No women participated in the first modern Olympic Games; but in 1900, eleven women took part in tennis and golf, the only two events open to them. Over the years, more and more women's events have been added. Athletes such as Shirley Babashoff, Donna de Varona, Mildred "Babe" Didrikson, Dorothy Hamill, Micki King, Florence Griffith Joyner, Janet Evans, and Wilma Rudolph have become international champions. In 1992, women participated in all events except baseball, boxing, soccer, weight lifting, wrestling, and the modern pentathlon.

Name _____

Women in the Olympics
Activity Sheet

1. On the lines below, make a list of six of the top women athletes of the past and the sports in which they excelled. Compare your list with the lists compiled by several of your friends. Circle the names that appear on more than one list. What characteristics do these outstanding women of yesterday have in common?

Women	**Sports**
1. _____	_____
2. _____	_____
3. _____	_____
4. _____	_____
5. _____	_____
6. _____	_____

2. On the lines below, make a list of six of the top women athletes of today and the sports in which they excel. Compare your list with the lists compiled by several of your friends. Circle the names that appear on more than one list. What characteristics do these outstanding women of today have in common?

Women	**Sports**
1. _____	_____
2. _____	_____
3. _____	_____
4. _____	_____
5. _____	_____
6. _____	_____

3. Women ran for the first time in an Olympic marathon in the 1984 Olympic Games in Los Angeles, California. Joan Benoit, an American athlete, won the race. Why were women banned from this race until 1984? What historical event does the marathon commemorate?

Name _____

Women Winners

Since they first began participating in the Olympic Games in 1900, women have given memorable performances in a variety of Olympic events. Each of the American women named in the left-hand column is associated with at least one Olympic sport listed in the right-hand column. Match the names with the sports by writing the correct letter on each line. If you need help, use an almanac or book of facts. You will need to use some letters more than once, and you will find that some women excelled in more than one sport.

_____ 1. Tenley Albright

_____ 2. Shirley Babashoff

_____ 3. Jenni Chandler

_____ 4. Donna de Varona

_____ 5. Mildred "Babe" Didrikson

_____ 6. Dorothy Hamill

_____ 7. Bonnie Blair

_____ 8. Micki King

_____ 9. Kristi Yamaguchi

_____ 10. Patricia McCormick

_____ 11. Debbie Meyer

_____ 12. Jackie Joyner-Kersee

_____ 13. Wilma Rudolph

_____ 14. Janet Evans

_____ 15. Wyomia Tyus

_____ 16. Joan Benoit

_____ 17. Luann Ryon

_____ 18. Mary Lou Retton

A. archery

B. figure skating

C. gymnastics

D. javelin throw

E. platform diving

F. running

G. speed skating

H. springboard diving

I. swimming

J. heptathlon

K. marathon runner

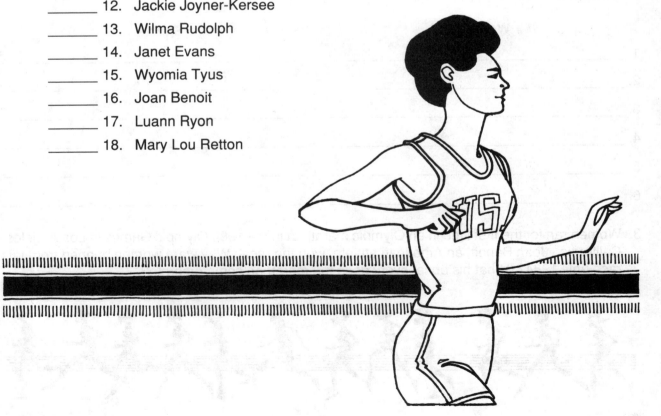

Name _____

Jackie Joyner-Kersee

The **heptathlon** is a grueling track and field competition that takes place over two days. It consists of seven events: the 100-meter hurdles, shot put, high jump, long jump, javelin, 200-meter race, and—providing the exciting finish to this Olympic event—the 800-meter race.

One American athlete has excelled in the requirements of the heptathlon—Jackie Joyner-Kersee. Her first try at the heptathlon was in the 1984 Olympic Games. She placed second, missing the gold medal by just five points. More determined than ever, she made a goal for herself to set a new Olympic record. Joyner-Kersee did even better. In the 1988 Olympics, she set a new record and also won the long jump, setting an Olympic record of 24 feet, $3\frac{1}{2}$ inches. Joyner-Kersee became the first woman to win consecutive heptathlon gold medals at the 1988 and 1992 Olympic Games.

Jacqueline Joyner was born in 1962 and began running at an early age, but it wasn't always easy. At the age of nine, she entered her first track competition, finishing last. When she was fourteen, she decided to train for the five-event pentathlon. In 1978, she won four National Junior Pentathlon championships. Joyner also excelled in academics and graduated in the top ten percent of her high school class. She continued her education at the University of California at Los Angeles, where she met and married Bob Kersee, a UCLA track coach who became her personal coach.

Activities

1. A five-event competition is called a pentathlon. Pentathlon is derived from the Greek words for five (*pente*) and contest (*athlon*).

   A seven-event competition is called a _____ .

   A ten-event competition is called a _____ .

   A three-event competition is called a _____ .

2. Jackie Joyner-Kersee combined a college education with an athletic career. Consider the reasons for combining athletics and education. Then write at least three reasons in support of this idea from three perspectives: a college teacher, an athletic coach, and a student-athlete.

3. If you were to organize an academic heptathlon, what subjects would you include?

Name _____

Mildred "Babe" Didrikson Zaharias

Among the most remembered women in the Olympics is Mildred "Babe" Didrikson Zaharias. Mildred grew up playing sandlot baseball with the boys in her Beaumont, Texas, neighborhood. She was good at their game. In fact, she was so good that her teammates nicknamed her "Babe." She reminded them of baseball star Babe Ruth.

As an athlete, Babe was not only incredibly capable, but also incredibly versatile. She played semiprofessional women's basketball and was three times named an All-American. She excelled in a variety of track and field events, won tennis tournaments and a diving championship, and had a bowling average of about 170.

Babe's genuine pride, brash wit, and unequaled athletic ability made her a favorite of the spectators who gathered in Los Angeles for the 1932 Olympic Games. Limited by Olympic rules to participating in only three events, she chose the 80-meter hurdles, the javelin throw, and the high jump. She won gold medals in the hurdle and javelin events. Although she tied the winner of the high jump, she was given a second-place silver medal because of her unorthodox jumping style in which her head sometimes went over the bar before her feet.

Name _____

Mildred "Babe" Didrikson Zaharias
(continued)

After the Olympics, Babe decided to turn professional. She played with a mixed women and men's basketball team and pitched for a men's baseball team. Then she decided to try golf and was soon winning both women's and men's tournaments.

In 1938, Babe Didrikson married George Zaharias, a prosperous wrestler and promoter. With his support, Babe could concentrate on her golf. She regained her amateur status by refusing to accept prize money for three years. She became the first American to win the British Women's Amateur Championship in 1947. In 1948, she turned pro again and joined with five others to found the Ladies Professional Golf Association.

In 1953, Babe began one last struggle against an opponent she could not defeat, cancer. Courageously, she fought back and within fifteen months, had won her third United States Open title by an unbelievable twelve strokes. But she could not defeat cancer. On September 27, 1956, Babe Didrikson Zaharias died. Women's athletics had lost a real champion.

Activities

1. During the 1930s, women might have played an occasional game of lawn tennis, but they certainly did *not* compete seriously in sports events. Babe Didrikson was different. As a result, people made fun of her and called her a "muscle moll." In an article entitled "I Blow My Own Horn," which appeared in the June 1936 issue of *American Magazine*, Babe wrote, "They seem to think I'm a strange, unnatural being. The idea seems to be that Muscle Molls are not people" (p. 104). People made fun of Babe because she was not like everyone else, not what they expected her to be. Have you ever made fun of someone who was different? How did doing so make you feel? How might it have made the other person feel? Has anyone ever made fun of you because you were different? How did this treatment make you feel?

2. Name the three Summer Olympic events that you think you would perform the best in, and explain which of your talents and skills caused you to name these particular events.

3. Create an all new Olympic event that is suited to your special talents and skills, one in which you would have a competitive edge. The event need not be strictly athletic. Structure the event carefully so that you are likely to win. Would you most enjoy competing if you were certain to win, or if you had a chance to win or lose depending on the effort you were willing to put forth? Why?

4. **Dressage, Fosbury flop**, and **steeplechase** are sports terms. Draw pictures of what you think these terms are, then look up their meanings.

Name _____

Who's Who in the Olympics?

Make your own Who's Who in the Olympics by investigating athletes who have competed in the Olympic Games, or will be competing in the upcoming games. You do not necessarily have to choose an athlete who won, or is expected to win, a gold medal. You might want to consider athletes who show outstanding sportsmanship or have overcome special challenges or hardships.

Event	Female Athlete and Country	Male Athlete and Country
archery		
badminton		
basketball		
canoeing		
cycling		
diving		
platform		
springboard		
equestrian events		
fencing		
field hockey		
gymnastics		
handball		
judo		
rowing		
shooting		

Name _____

Who's Who in the Olympics?
(continued)

Event	Female Athlete and Country	Male Athlete and Country
swimming		
synchronized swimming		
table tennis		
tennis		
track and field		
discus throw		
high jump		
javelin throw		
long jump		
decathlon (men)		
heptathlon (women)		
running		
100 meters		
200 meters		
400 meters		
800 meters		
1,500 meters		
100-meter hurdles		
400-meter hurdles		
marathon		
shot put		

Name _____

Greg Louganis

Greg Louganis was the diver to beat in the springboard and platform diving events at the 1988 Olympic Games. Four years earlier, at the Los Angeles Olympics, he had easily won gold medals in both of these events. The games in Seoul were to be the last Olympic competition of his long career.

As Louganis stepped onto the springboard, he felt confident. He had performed the reverse $2\frac{1}{2}$ somersault over 200,000 times. Yet, this time, Louganis misjudged his jump. As he came out of his first somersault, the top of his head whacked the board. Louganis fell into the water with a heavy splash. When he came to the surface, his head was bleeding and his confidence was shaken.

His poor dive dropped him from first to fifth place. Patched up with temporary stitches, Louganis stepped onto the diving board for the next round of dives. Summoning all his courage, he attempted one of his most difficult dives. The judges awarded him the highest score of the competition, which qualified him for the finals the next day.

For the finals, Louganis had to perform the same dive that caused him to hit his head the day before. He was unusually tense for this final round. He had only a slender seven-point lead over his nearest competitor, Liangke Tan of China. As the crowd watched in silence, he began his dive. Seconds later he pierced the water, making a spectacular dive. Two rounds later, he had earned his gold medal.

Then Greg had to switch his focus to the last diving competition of his Olympic career—platform diving. His toughest competition was a fourteen-year-old Chinese diver, Ni Xiong. Throughout each round, they were in a very tight race. It would take a near-perfect dive for Greg to beat this young challenger. He planned to try a reverse $3\frac{1}{2}$ somersault, sometimes called the "death dive." This dive is named for the Soviet diver Sergei Shalibashvili, who died attempting it in an international competition. Louganis poised himself at the top of the platform, rose on his toes, then pushed himself up and away from the tower. When the judges' scores were added up, Louganis broke into tears of joy and relief. He had survived incredible pressure to win his final gold medal by slightly more than one point!

Name _____

Greg Louganis
Activity Sheet

1. Although Louganis made it look easy, he found it difficult to cope with the mental pressure of a sport where so much time was spent waiting, and the dive took only a few seconds. In the 1984 Olympics, he was given a stuffed bear for good luck by his coach's wife. He chose to talk to the bear in private to calm himself down and to build up his confidence. What are some times when you are scared and need to have your confidence built up? When you are in these situations, what do you do? Talk to other people to find out what techniques they use.

2. Louganis has a theater arts degree from the University of California at Irvine. Pretend that his assignment is to write a play about an unusual diving competition in an Olympics of the future. Make a list of the characters that he might have in his play and include a short description of each.

3. Greg Louganis is regarded by many as the greatest diver in history. He gained this reputation when he was only twenty-four years old. Most people do not achieve their goals until they are much older. What are some of the goals you have set for yourself for the future?

Name _____

Oksana Baiul

Representing the Ukraine in the 1992 Olympics, sixteen-year-old Oksana Baiul skated to a gold medal in spite of a lifetime of hardships. When she was thirteen, Oksana's mother died. Her father had deserted the family years before, so Oksana was left without family members to turn to for help. She spent the next year living with her coach and his family, but he emigrated to Canada to seek a better future than the Ukraine could offer him. Once again, Oksana was on her own. At this difficult time, Galina Zmievskaya, the coach for Viktor Petrenko (1992 Olympic gold-medal winner) took over. She included Oksana in her family as a third daughter. During the next several years, Oksana quickly leapt from one victory to another. According to skating experts, she has the expressive arms and flexibility of a ballet dancer, and is one of the most "musical" skaters to compete in a long time. Since her victory in the 1992 Olympics, Oksana has become a celebrity and has toured many cities around the world and in the United States.

Activities

1. One of the reasons that Oksana's coach left was because Canada could offer him more advantages than the Ukraine could. Research the recent history of the Ukraine and write a short report about it. What were the competitors called in the 1988 Olympics who skated for countries in the former Soviet Union?

2. In figure skating certain moves are named for their inventors. The **axel**, a jump made as a skater moves forward, is named for Axel Paulsen. The **lutz**, another difficult jump and turn, is named for Alois Lutz, and the **salchow**, a jump and turn where the skater takes off on one foot and lands on the other, is named for 1908 Olympic gold medalist Ulrich Salchow. Think about the ice skating events that you have seen. Then invent a difficult maneuver that includes unique spins, turns, lifts, or jumps. Make a drawing of the different parts of the move. Finally, name the move for yourself!

Name _____

Olympic Fashions

Have you ever seen a hockey goalie dressed for a game? You probably did not think that the clothes the goalie was wearing were particularly fashionable, but the outfit makes more sense when you watch a hockey game and see the goalie in action. The goalie *needs* that mask and all of that padding as protection against waving sticks and flying pucks. The goalie's uniform is designed primarily to be practical, to serve a purpose—that of protection.

Like other sports fashions, Olympic fashions are influenced by practicality, but tradition and technology also play a part. Tradition dictates the clothing worn for some sports, such as the equestrian events, and it has changed very little over the years. Technology has influenced the clothing worn for other sports, because competitors have discovered that modifications in clothing and equipment can improve their performances.

In one instance, technology even contributed to the creation of an entirely new sport. Until the late 1800s, the only kind of skiing was cross-country, or Nordic, skiing. When improvements in buckle and binding design made it possible to attach ski boots more securely to skis, skiers were able to ski down steep mountain slopes without losing their skis, and Alpine, or downhill, skiing was born.

Besides the special clothing Olympic athletes wear to compete, the entire Olympic team from each country has an official uniform that team members wear at the opening and closing ceremonies. This colorful uniform is especially created for the Olympics. Its design is usually influenced by the heritage or native costume of the country whose team member wears it.

Name _____

Olympic Fashions
Activity Sheet

1. On the lines below, list two or three Olympic sports for which major clothing changes have been made to improve performance. Then, briefly describe the change and, if possible, give the Olympic year in which the new version first appeared. Or, if you prefer, select one sport, such as swimming, and document by Olympic year the changes that have been made in the clothing worn for that particular sport. You may need to use the photographs in old newspapers and magazines to complete your research.

Sport	Clothing Change
_____	_____
_____	_____
_____	_____
_____	_____
_____	_____
_____	_____

2. After investigating the cultural heritage of a country, design an official uniform for athletes from that country to wear during the opening and closing Olympic ceremonies.

Name _____

Compare What They Wear

1. Look at the athletes pictured below. Study their special clothing carefully. Decide what Olympic sport each is dressed for. Write the name of that sport on the line provided.

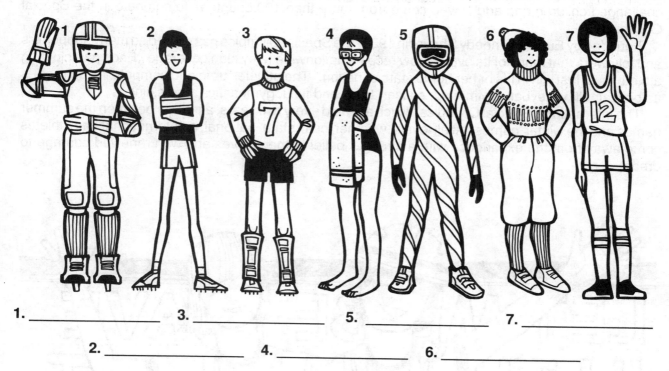

1. _____   3. _____   5. _____   7. _____

2. _____   4. _____   6. _____

2. Figure skating outfits have changed quite a bit in the fifty-six years since Sonja Henie first delighted Olympic spectators. Compare the clothes worn in 1928 with those worn now. Check books on costumes, ice skating, and the Olympic Games to gather information. In what ways are they alike? In what ways are they different? What fashion trends and technological developments have influenced these changes? Design an ice skating costume suitable for a skater in the Olympics 100 years from now.

Name _____

The Special Olympics

There is one group of athletes who exhibits as much courage, spirit, and dedication as the athletes who participate in the International Olympic Games. These athletes are the mentally or physically challenged children and adults who come from more than 100 countries to compete in the Special Olympics.

Founded by Eunice Kennedy Shriver in 1968, the Special Olympics has gained so many supporters and followers that many of its events now receive nationwide television coverage. Each participating athlete must first win in his or her home state or nation. The athletes train and compete in such sports as basketball, volleyball, swimming, soccer, track and field, gymnastics, and skiing.

The International Special Olympics, which are held every two years, alternate between the summer games and the winter games. At all levels, whether local, state, national, or international, the athletes come away from the experience with a stronger belief in themselves and with renewed courage to dream.

Activities

1. As a member of the news media covering the Special Olympics, you have been asked to interview a member of the winning soccer team. Make a list of the questions that you will ask this athlete. Then write the article and include the remarks that a coach or spectator made concerning the personal qualities and level of effort it took to compete.

2. Does your community or state sponsor Special Olympic Games? Write for information on ways you and your friends can help at Special Olympics events. Address your inquiries to Special Olympics International, 1350 New York Avenue NW, Washington, DC 20005.

3. Pretend that you are the physical activities director for the United States Association for Blind Athletes. You have been asked to create a new team sporting event that would be appropriate for blind children. Use existing special equipment (balls with beepers, for example), or invent something entirely new. Make a drawing which includes the special equipment and its use.

Amateur—To Be or Not to Be?

The definition of *amateur athletics* has been an ongoing problem for the International Olympic Committee. The phrase **amateur athlete** means someone who engages in a sport for enjoyment rather than for money. Until recently, participants in the Olympic Games were supposed to be amateurs. According to the Olympic by-laws, participants could accept academic scholarships, teach physical education, and receive assistance from their National Olympic committee for the costs of immediate preparation and actual competition. On the other hand, they could not receive continual payments from a single agency or otherwise benefit materially by their athletic skill.

What appears to be a simple rule of "no professionals" has not been easy to enforce. The problem is that different countries interpret the rules differently. In many countries, the training of athletes is supervised and supported by the government. Very young children with talent and promise are given intensive training paid for entirely by the government. In some countries "amateur" athletes are given government jobs as customs officials, fire fighters, or military personnel, but are not required to work. This arrangement gives them an advantage in that they do not need to earn a living and have almost unlimited time to train. This inconsistent enforcement of the rules creates a hardship on athletes who receive no direct government subsidy and have to support themselves.

Something had to change. The International Olympic Committee decided to replace the term "amateur" with the term "eligible athlete," and gave the governing body for each sport the power to set the eligibility rules for its sport. Even though some sports still allow only amateurs to participate in the Olympics, the trend toward "eligible athlete" was seen at the Olympics in Seoul. By the 1992 Olympics in Barcelona, professional athletes were openly welcomed. Payment to U.S. athletes can come in the form of prize money, trust funds, direct cash payments, and job opportunities. Regardless of the sport, athletes do not receive monetary awards as a prize for winning in the Olympic Games.

Activities

1. In 1992, the U.S. Olympic Basketball Federation allowed professional players to be members of the Olympic team. This decision was controversial. Do you think it was the right decision? Make a list of the reasons for your opinion. Debate your position with a friend of a differing opinion.

2. Look up the derivation of the word **amateur**. How does the meaning of this word's Latin root relate to its English definition?

3. What would you do if you were an amateur athlete and found yourself being offered a substantial sum of money to endorse a product or to sign a contract for a professional sports team?

Name _____

Jim Thorpe

The **decathlon** is one of the most difficult Olympic events. It is the supreme test of an athlete's stamina and skill. Each participant in the decathlon must compete in ten separate track and field events. These events are the high jump, the long jump, the javelin and discus throws, the pole vault, the shot put, the 110-meter high hurdles, and the 100-meter, 400-meter, and 1,500-meter runs. All ten events must be completed on two successive days. Points are awarded to an athlete for each event on the basis of how close he comes to equaling the world record for that event. At the end of decathlon competition, the competitor who has earned the most points is declared the winner.

James Francis Thorpe was born near Prague, Oklahoma, in 1888. His mother, a Sac Indian, named him Bright Path, but most people just called him Jim. Jim's father was a rancher who worked hard and enjoyed strenuous exercise. He encouraged his sons to develop their running and throwing skills. He also urged them to get a good education.

In 1907, Jim entered the Carlisle Indian School in Carlisle, Pennsylvania. One year later, he joined the Carlisle football team coached by Glenn "Pop" Warner. During the 1911–12 season, Warner and his left halfback, Jim Thorpe, led Carlisle to upset victories over such highly rated teams as Army, Harvard, and the University of Pennsylvania.

In 1912, Jim Thorpe took part in the Olympic Games at Stockholm, Sweden. He competed in both the pentathlon and the decathlon, and astounded everyone with his speed and skill. He won the broad jump (now called the long jump) and the 200- and 1,500-meter runs of the pentathlon; won the shot put, the 1,500-meter run, and the hurdle race of the decathlon; and was the runner-up in all of the other pentathlon and decathlon events. His performance was so outstanding that he won first place in both events and was awarded two gold medals. In addition, he received special honors from the King of Sweden, who called him "the greatest athlete in the world," and was welcomed as a hero when he returned to the United States.

Name _____

Jim Thorpe
(continued)

But Jim Thorpe's victories were short-lived. During the 1909–10 season, he had played semi-professional baseball with the Rocky Mountain, North Carolina team, and had received a small amount of money for doing so. Thus, when he competed in the Olympics, he was not an amateur in the strictest sense. In 1913, at the request of the Amateur Athletic Union and at the insistence of Glenn Warner, Jim Thorpe surrendered his awards to the International Olympic headquarters in Switzerland.

Activities

1. Do you think that Jim Thorpe should have been asked to give up his medals? Why or why not?

2. Jim Thorpe died in 1953. After his death, members of his family sought to have his performance officially recognized and his medals returned. Finally, in 1982, the awards Jim Thorpe surrendered were returned to his survivors and the official Olympic record now lists Thorpe among the 1912 winners. Refer to biographies and sports books in the library to learn about the Thorpe family's long struggle and victory.

3. Since Jim Thorpe's decathlon victory in 1912, athletes from the United States have won this grueling competition nine times. Choose one of the following U.S. decathlon winners: James Bausch, Milton Campbell, Bruce Jenner, Rafer Johnson, Robert Mathias, Glenn Morris, Harold Osborn, and Bill Toomey. Read about this athlete's participation in the Olympics. Then pretend that you are a reporter and write an eyewitness account of the athlete's experiences at the games.

Name _____

World's Fastest Human

Jesse Owens was born in 1915 in rural Alabama, where his family struggled to make a living as sharecroppers. Every year, young Jesse was sick most of the winter with colds and a lingering cough. Thinking that a change might improve Jesse's health and better the family's financial condition, Jesse's father decided to move north to Cleveland, Ohio. The change not only improved Jesse's health, but also brought him in contact with the world of track and with a coach who took an interest in helping Jesse develop his special skills.

Jesse's skills were special indeed. He won the broad jump (now called the long jump) titles at the outdoor (1933–34) and indoor (1934–35) meets of the National Amateur Athletic Union. The next year, as a member of the Ohio State University track team, he broke several world records in broad jumping, hurdle racing, and flat racing.

At the 1936 Olympic competition in Berlin, Jesse Owens astounded spectators by equaling the world mark in the 100-meter race, by breaking world records in the 200-meter race and the broad jump, and by winning (with Ralph Metcalfe) the 400-meter relay. Altogether, Jesse Owens, an African-American member of the U.S. Olympic team, won four gold medals and earned the unofficial title of "World's Fastest Human."

Activities

1. In 1936, Jesse Owens ran the 200-meter race in 20.7 seconds. In 1984, Carl Lewis ran the race in 19.80 seconds, and, in 1992, Mike Marsh ran the same race in 20.01 seconds. What conditions might influence the speed of a runner? Compare the training of an athlete in 1936 with that of an athlete of today.

2. Pretend you are a reporter sent to Berlin to report on the Olympic Games. Your editor has requested a feature article on the "Jesse Owens story." Make a list of ten important points that you intend to include in your article.

3. In 1984, Carl Lewis of the United States equalled Jesse Owens' accomplishment by winning four gold medals. Read about these two world-class athletes. What were the similarities and differences between their Olympic performances? Write a short story about what you think Carl Lewis was thinking when he was standing on the victory platform hearing the "Star Spangled Banner" for the fourth time.

Name _____

Who Wins the Olympics?

The Olympics is a contest among athletes and not among countries. The International Olympic Committee insists that individual effort and excellence are what is important and that overall national achievement has little meaning. For this reason, they decided not to keep an official score among the competing nations; in other words, no nation "wins" the Olympics.

However, the international press assigns different numbers of points to the gold, silver, and bronze medals won by each country and is able to obtain an overall score for each nation. They name an unofficial national winner for the Olympic Games. Many newspaper and television reporters believe that people want to know about the accomplishments of different countries. They say they feel obligated to identify winners by country and to report national medal totals.

Activity

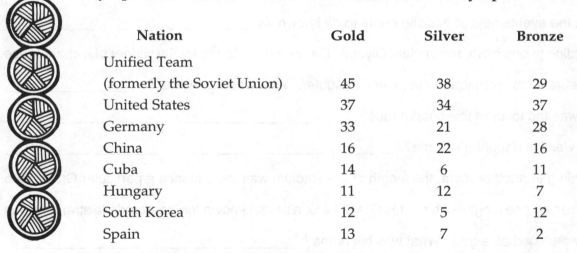

Olympic Medal Distribution for the 1992 Summer Olympic Games

Nation	Gold	Silver	Bronze
Unified Team (formerly the Soviet Union)	45	38	29
United States	37	34	37
Germany	33	21	28
China	16	22	16
Cuba	14	6	11
Hungary	11	12	7
South Korea	12	5	12
Spain	13	7	2

1. Pretend that you are a newspaper reporter. Your readers want to know who "won" the Olympics. Using the chart above, assign three points for every gold medal, two points for every silver medal, and one point for every bronze medal. Add up the points for each country. Who "won" the Olympics in 1992? Now that you have this information, write the article highlighting the countries that did well, but also include information about the official IOC viewpoint on "national winners."

2. Do you think the emphasis in the coverage of the most recent Olympic Games was on individual achievement or on a medal count for each country? What would you do to improve television coverage of the Olympic Games?

Name _____

Olympic Treasure Hunt

    See how quickly you can answer these fifty questions about the Olympics. Some of the information you need appears on the pages in this book, but some of it does not. You will need to look up this information elsewhere. See page 47 for ideas about where to look.

1. Who were the twelve Olympians? _____

    _____

2. Where did they live? _____

3. Name any six of the twelve Olympians.

    _____   _____

    _____   _____

    _____   _____

4. The Greeks chose a plain in Elis called _____ as one site for religious celebrations and athletic contests in honor of these gods.

5. Later, the events held at this site came to be known as _____ .

6. According to one myth, the ancient Olympic Games were started by the winner of a chariot race to celebrate his marriage to the loser's daughter. Who was the winner? _____

7. Who was the loser of this chariot race? _____

8. What was his daughter's name? _____

9. According to another myth, the length of the stadium was the distance a particular Greek hero could run on one lungful of air. This Greek hero, a mortal known for his incredible strength, was later worshiped as a god. What was his name? _____

10. The first recorded Olympic Games were held in the year _____ .

Name _____

Olympic Treasure Hunt
(continued)

11. The winner of the only event held during these first games was a runner by the name of _____ from the city of _____ .

12. During the first fifty-two years of the ancient Olympic Games, a _____ over the full length of the stadium was the only event.

13. In the ancient Olympic Games, what was a winning athlete's only official reward? _____

    _____

14. Who do many historians believe was the greatest hero of the ancient Olympic Games?

    _____

15. In which sport did he excel? _____

16. How did he develop his astounding strength? _____

    _____

17. Polydamas was champion of an ancient Olympic event called the **pancratium**. This name comes from the Greek word *pankrates*. What does this Greek word mean? _____

18. The pancratium was intended to prepare men for battle. This ancient Olympic event involved skills now used in two modern Olympic sports. Name these two modern sports.

    _____   _____

19. Arrachion of Phigalia won the pancratium under somewhat unusual circumstances. What were they? _____

    _____

    _____

    _____

Name _____

Olympic Treasure Hunt
(continued)

20. Official written records were not kept during the early days of the ancient Olympic Games, and there were no newspapers in which the outcomes of each day's contests could be reported. Name five sources from which modern scholars have learned about the ancient Olympic Games.

    _____

    _____

    _____

    _____

    _____

21. Women were not allowed to participate in the ancient Olympic Games or even to watch them. As early as the sixth century B.C., Greek women began holding games of their own. What were these games called? _____

22. Whom did these games honor? _____

23. In what year were the ancient Olympic Games stopped? _____

24. Who stopped them?_____

25. Why were they stopped? _____

    _____

    _____

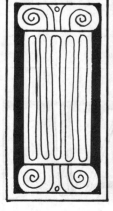  

Name _____

Olympic Treasure Hunt
(continued)

26. What was the name of the French nobleman who worked during the 1800s to revive the Olympic Games? _____

27. When and where were the first modern Olympic Games held?_____

28. How many years passed between the last ancient Olympic Games and the first modern ones?

    _____

29. How many nations sent competing athletes to the first modern Olympic Games? _____

30. In what nine events did these athletes compete?

    _____   _____   _____

    _____   _____   _____

    _____   _____   _____

31. The white Olympic flag bears the Olympic symbol, five interlocking rings. These rings symbolize the five participating continents. Name these five continents.

    _____   _____

    _____   _____

    _____

32. What colors are these five rings?

    _____   _____   _____

    _____   _____

33. The motto for the Olympic Games is *Citius, Altius, Fortius*. What do these three Latin words mean? _____

34. What woman finished with two gold medals and a silver in the women's track events in the 1992 Barcelona Games? _____

35. At which Olympic Games were both singles and doubles badminton competitions awarded full medal status?_____

Name _____

Olympic Treasure Hunt
(continued)

36. In what year did women first compete in the Olympic Games? _____

37. Among the most remembered women in the modern Olympics is Mildred "Babe" Didrikson Zaharias. During the 1932 Olympic Games in Los Angeles, she won gold medals in two events. What were they? _____

38. For what non-Olympic sport is Babe best known? _____

39. Which team has won the most gold medals in the women's gymnastic competitions?

    _____

40. At the 1968 Olympic Games in Mexico City, a fifteen-year-old American gymnast placed sixteenth in the women's all-round competition, far better than any United States woman gymnast had ever done before. What was her name? _____

41. During the 1976 Olympics in Montreal, a young girl on the Romanian team earned the first perfect score in Olympic gymnastic competition. What was her name? _____

42. A woman diver from the United States won the Olympic competition in both springboard and platform diving in 1952 and again in 1956. What was her name? _____

43. In the 1960 Olympics, an African-American woman beat her competitors in the 100-meter run, the 200-meter run, and the 400-meter relay to win three gold medals. Her accomplishment was all the more remarkable because she first had to beat the effects of a crippling disease called polio. What was this remarkable runner's name? _____

44. In the 1912 Olympic Games at Stockholm, Sweden, an American Indian won first place in both the pentathlon and the decathlon and was called "the greatest athlete in the world" by the King of Sweden. What was this athlete's name? _____

45. What American won the gold medal for the discus throw in 1952, 1956, 1960, and 1964?

    _____

Name _____

Olympic Treasure Hunt
(continued)

46. At the 1936 Olympic competition in Berlin, an American earned four gold medals and the unofficial title of "World's Fastest Human." What was the athlete's name? _____

47. The 1992 Games in Barcelona marked the first time that both amateur and professional basketball players represented the U.S. in Olympic competition. Name three of the twelve National Basketball Association players who competed on this Olympic team. _____

_____

48. Bruce Jenner, Rafer Johnson, Robert Mathias, and Bill Toomey are all winners of which Olympic event? _____

49. What American swimmer won an unprecedented seven individual and team gold medals in Olympic competition in 1972? _____

50. Name the woman who won gold medals in swimming in both the 1988 and 1992 Olympic Games.

_____

For Additional Information About the Olympics

Read:

Arlott, John, ed. *The Oxford Companion to World Sports and Games.* NY: Oxford University Press, 1975.

Durant, John. *Highlights of the Olympics: From Ancient Times to the Present.* 5th ed. NY: Hastings House, 1977.

Finley, Moses I., and H. W. Pleket. *The Olympic Games: The First Thousand Years.* NY: Viking Press, 1976.

Glubok, Shirley, and Alfred Tamarin. *Olympic Games in Ancient Greece.* NY: Harper & Row, 1976.

Jenner, Bruce, and Phillip Finch. *Decathlon Challenge: Bruce Jenner's Story.* Englewood Cliffs, NJ: Prentice-Hall, 1977.

Johnson, William O. *All That Glitters Is Not Gold: The Olympic Games.* NY: Putnam, 1972.

Menke, Frank Grant. *Encyclopedia of Sports.* Indianapolis, IN: A. S. Barnes, 1978.

Page, James A. *Black Olympian Medalists.* Englewood, CO: Libraries Unlimited, Inc., 1991.

Wallechinsky, David. *The Complete Book of the Olympics*, 1992 Edition. NY: Penguin Books, 1991.

The World Almanac and Book of Facts 1995. NY: St. Martins Press, 1994.

Write To:
United States Olympic Committee
One Olympic Plaza
Colorado Springs, CO 80909

Name _____

Olympic Metrics

In the ancient Olympic Games, measurements were not important. There were no weight classifications for wrestling or boxing, distances were not measured, and times were not kept. Winning was all that mattered. In the modern Olympic Games, measurements are all-important. Times and distances are the means by which achievement is evaluated and records are set or broken.

At the Olympics, the metric system of measurement is used. This is a decimal system based on the meter. The English word **meter** comes from the Greek word *metron*, meaning "measure." A meter is expressed as fractions or multiples of one meter. For example, a **kilometer** is one thousand meters, and a millimeter is one-thousandth of a meter.

Use what you know about the metric system to answer these questions. If you need additional information, consult the measurement tables in a dictionary or mathematics textbook and/or the distance tables in an almanac or atlas.

1. What metric unit would you use to measure the diameter of a discus? _____

2. What metric unit would you use to measure the length of a javelin? _____

3. What metric unit would you use to measure the length of a Nordic ski course? _____

4. Is the 100-meter dash longer or shorter than the 100-yard dash? _____

   By how many yards? _____

5. If the world record for the 100-yard dash is 9.0 seconds, would you expect the Olympic record for

   the 100-meter dash to be slightly longer or slightly shorter? _____

6. What Olympic race would be closest in length to the one-mile run? _____

7. Is this race shorter or longer than a mile? _____

   By how many yards? _____

8. If you traveled from New York City to Los Angeles to attend the Olympics, would the distance you

   traveled be closest to 4,500 centimeters, 4,500 meters, or 4,500 kilometers? _____

9. Approximately what distance would you travel in highway miles if you made this cross-country trip

   through St. Louis, Missouri? _____

10. The usual course for a marathon is 26 miles, 385 yards. What metric units would you use to

    express this distance? _____

    How long would the course be in these units? _____

Name _____

Graphing the Games

A **graph** is a line or diagram that shows how one quantity depends on or changes with another quantity. A graph makes a comparison or shows a system of relationships in a way that is easy to understand. Among the various kinds of graphs are bar graphs, circle graphs, line graphs, and picture graphs.

The box at the bottom of the page lists the distances for some of the winning jumps in Olympic long jump competition. Represent this information on the grid in bar or line graph form.

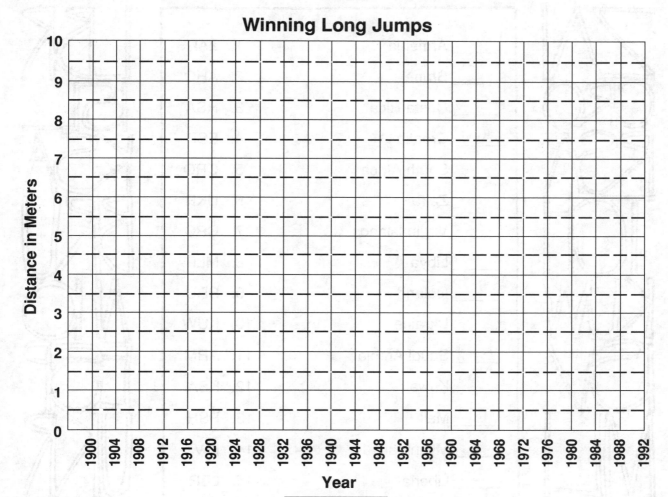

Winning Long Jumps

Distance in Meters

Year

Distances

Year	Distance	Year	Distance	Year	Distance
1900	7.19 meters	1932	7.64	1964	8.12
1904	7.35	1936	8.06	1968	8.90
1908	7.48	1940	no games	1972	8.24
1912	7.60	1944	no games	1976	8.35
1916	no games	1948	7.25	1980	8.54
1920	7.15	1952	7.57	1984	8.54
1924	7.45	1956	7.83	1988	8.72
1928	7.73	1960	8.12	1992	8.67

Name _____

Can You Identify the IOC Abbreviations?

In 1992, 172 countries participated in the Olympic Games. By 1993, 194 countries and territories were recognized by the International Olympic Committee. The IOC assigns each an abbreviation. Match the countries and their abbreviations by writing the number of the abbreviation, found in the right-hand column, on the line in front of the correct country. Then test your geography skills by locating the countries listed below on a map or globe.

_____ Armenia	1.	ZAI
_____ Brunei	2.	AHO
_____ Costa Rica	3.	RSA
_____ Croatia	4.	ESP
_____ South Africa	5.	CRO
_____ Zaire	6.	UKR
_____ Virgin Islands	7.	CRC
_____ Libya	8.	MLI
_____ Iceland	9.	BRU
_____ Ukraine	10.	KUW
_____ Saudi Arabia	11.	ARM
_____ Kuwait	12.	KSA
_____ Mali	13.	BSH
_____ Myanmar	14.	ISV
_____ Liberia	15.	LBR
_____ Czech Republic	16	LBA
_____ Spain	17	MYA
_____ Puerto Rico	18	TCH
_____ Bosnia-Herzegovina	19.	ISL
_____ Netherlands Antilles	20.	PUR

Name _____

Olympic Controversies

In ancient Greece, soldiers stopped battles between city-states to participate in the Olympic Games. In modern times, the Olympic games are meant to cross political boundaries and rise above nationalistic self-interest.

Despite the high ideals of the Olympics, the games have often been controversial and a target for criticism. Below are some of the times when the Olympics have been used for political purposes:

- **1948 Olympics:** the Japanese, German, and Italian athletes were barred from the games in London, even though World War II had ended three years before.

- **1970 Olympics:** South Africa was excluded from the Olympic Games because of its practice of apartheid. In 1992, they were reinstated.

- **1972 Olympics:** Arab terrorists attacked the quarters of the Israeli team. Eleven Israeli hostages, five terrorists, and a West German policeman died in the attack.

- **1976 and 1980 Olympics:** the Taiwanese athletes, formerly representing "nationalist" China, were not allowed to compete under the flag of China. Representatives from China could only be from the People's Republic of China. Now the Taiwanese are recognized as athletes from Chinese Taipei.

- **1980 Olympics:** the United States, Canada, and fifty-two other countries refused to participate in the Olympic Games held in Moscow as a protest against the Soviet Union's invasion of Afghanistan in 1979 and 1980.

- **1984 Olympics:** the Soviet Union and fourteen other nations boycotted the Games in Los Angeles because they felt there would be poor security arrangements.

- **1988 Olympics:** Cuba and North Korea boycotted the Games because they were being held in Seoul, South Korea.

Name _____

Olympic Controversies
(continued)

Activities

1. Many Olympic athletes had trained for over four years and were at their peak performance level when the United States announced the boycott of the Moscow Games to protest the Soviet Union's invasion of Afghanistan. There were many athletes who supported the United States government in its protest against the Soviet Union, and there were many who desired to participate in the Olympics. Imagine that you are an athlete ready to participate in the 1980 Olympics. In the space below, write a letter to President Jimmy Carter expressing your opinion on the boycott. Explain why you either support or do not support the decision.

2. Olympic athletes know they must avoid illegal drugs such as marijuana, cocaine, and heroin, as well as drugs used to enhance athletic performance and physical appearance. In the 1988 Summer Games, ten athletes were disqualified for using banned drugs to increase their performance. One athlete, Ben Johnson from Canada, had to forfeit his gold medal in the 100-meter dash because tests showed the presence of anabolic steroids (used to enhance performance) in his blood. What recommendations can you make to the IOC for ensuring that the Olympic Games are drug-free?

3. Choose one of the controversies outlined on page 51. Find out more details about the incident. First, take the role of an International Olympic Committee member and write to the head of a country involved in the controversy. Explain why the Olympic ideals should take precedence over political concerns. Next, write a response from the head of this country.

Name _____

Summer Games on Water

Canoeing

Two types of boats are used in the canoeing event: **kayaks** and **canoes**. Both canoeing and kayaking were a means of transportation before they were considered as an event for the Olympics. The first kayaks were made thousands of years ago by Eskimos who used them to hunt and fish. They were made out of seal skins that were stretched over a frame of bone or wood and waterproofed with whale fat. They were extremely agile and seaworthy. The West Indian people of the Pacific northwest devised a lighter weight canoe made from birchbark which could navigate river currents and carry large loads.

Men's canoeing first appeared at the 1936 Berlin Games, with canoers from nineteen nations competing. At the 1948 London Games, one event was included for women. In modern Olympic Games, two types of competitions are held which are classified first by the type of water in which they are raced, and then by the type of boat. They are open to both men and women. The **flatwater sprint** is a short-distance event where women race for 500 meters and men race for 500 and 1,000 meters. The race is held on the smooth water of a lake or channel. **Whitewater slalom** competitions take place on a fast-moving river and competitors must paddle their boats around a series of gates, such as those found on a slalom ski course. Although the race is patterned after a run on a torrential river in the wilderness, most Olympic courses are man-made with natural-type rapids built into the course.

Both kayaks and canoes are entered in the flatwater sprints and whitewater slalom. Olympic canoes and kayaks are made out of fiberglass, aluminum, or an extremely tough synthetic fiber called kevlar, which is molded into the appropriate shape. The most noticeable difference between a flatwater and a whitewater boat is length. Flatwater boats are longer and more sleekly constructed, with V-shaped hulls designed for speed. The whitewater boats are more compact so they can be easily maneuvered. They have a flattened, more rounded hull. Whitewater athletes wear a flotation device and a helmet. The boat is "decked" or covered with an elastic fabric which is stretched tightly over the boat. The covering creates a watertight seal around the cockpit which prevents water from filling the boat during competition. The opening in the covering is called a porthole and that is where the paddler sits.

Name _____

Summer Games on Water
(continued)

Canoeing (continued)

Several things distinguish kayak paddlers from canoe paddlers. One is their position in the boat. Canoe paddlers kneel. In whitewater races, they kneel on both knees and rest their hips against the thwarts (seats). In flatwater races, they usually use the high kneel position, kneeling on one knee with the other leg placed in front for leverage. Kayak paddlers sit in the boat with their legs extended before them. Another way to distinguish the two is by the type of paddle that is used. Canoers use a single-bladed paddle, while a double-bladed paddle is used by kayakers.

Canoeing Activities

1. In the section on canoeing, you read about canoes and kayaks. How many other kinds of water vehicles can you think of? Compare your list with a friend's. What was the total number? (Examples: raft, passenger ship, submarine)

2. Use your innovative thinking skills and come up with an improvement on the design of the kayak. Give some thought to what would make the kayak more seaworthy, easier to maneuver, or more comfortable for the paddler. Make a drawing of your new kayak and label the changes you made.

3. Choose a type of water in which you would like to race (flatwater or whitewater) and a boat (either a kayak or a canoe). Then, using your choices, write a paragraph about a close competition with a rival athlete. Include detailed descriptions of the water, the way your boat is handling the location and conditions, and your thoughts as you struggle to win the race.

Name _____

Summer Games on Water
(continued)

Rowing

Rowing races have been around for a long time. The ancient Chinese held longboat races, and the ancient Egyptians raced open barges on the Nile. The Greeks began racing about 2,000 years ago and discovered that they could increase their rowing efficiency by mounting their paddles to the side of their boat. The first recorded rowing race in Europe was held on the Thames River in London in 1716.

Rowing has been a part of the Summer Olympics since 1976 for women and 1990 for men. Rowing competitions are held on flat water. There are two kinds of rowing events: **sweeps** and **sculls**. The sweep is done with both hands on one oar. Sculling is done with two oars—one oar in each hand. In both events, rowers sit facing backward and pull the oars, which are mounted on the side of the boat

Sculling competitors are divided into single sculls with one rower, double sculls with two rowers, and quadruple sculls for four rowers. Sweep races are open to pairs, fours, and eights. Usually there is an extra crew member called a **coxswain** in sweep races. The coxswain sits facing forward at the very back of the boat and steers by using a hand control that is attached to a rudder. The coxswain also calls out to the rowers to keep them rowing together.

Summer Games on Water
(continued)

Rowing

The boats that are used in rowing are called **shells**. They are made of fiberglass or carbon fiber. Some shells are constructed with hulls that are only 1/16th of an inch thick. The shells are designed to glide through the water smoothly. Rowers sit on sliding seats in the boats. They lace their feet into shoes mounted in front of them. On each stroke, the rower pushes off with her feet, moving the seat backward while pulling the oar through the water.

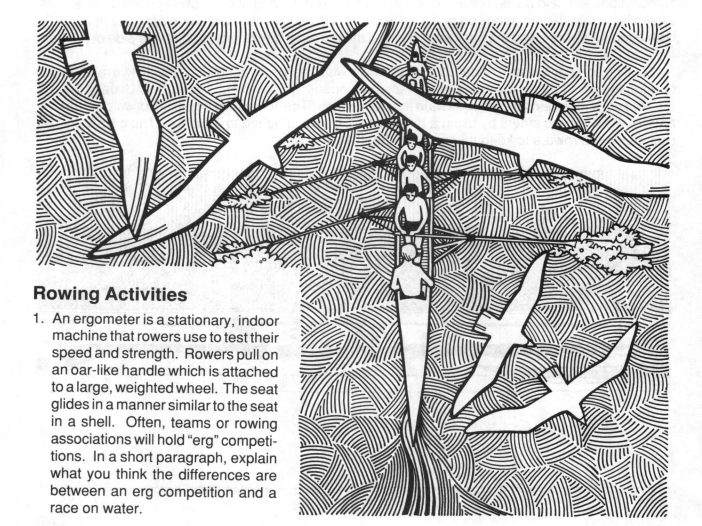

Rowing Activities

1. An ergometer is a stationary, indoor machine that rowers use to test their speed and strength. Rowers pull on an oar-like handle which is attached to a large, weighted wheel. The seat glides in a manner similar to the seat in a shell. Often, teams or rowing associations will hold "erg" competitions. In a short paragraph, explain what you think the differences are between an erg competition and a race on water.

2. Anne Marden is considered one of the best American rowers. Her specialty is the sculls. She won silver medals in the 1984 and 1988 Olympics. Using reference materials such as Olympic and sports almanacs, make a list of other rowers from the United States and other countries. Which countries seem to dominate in rowing events?

Name _____

Summer Games on Water
(continued)

Yachting

The sailing competition at the Summer Olympics is called yachting. Sailing has been an Olympic sport since the 1896 Athens Games, although the yacht racing events had to be canceled due to stormy weather. Women's events were added for the 1988 Seoul Games. The 1908 Olympic Games marked the only time an event was held for motorized boats. Today, there are events for eight types of boats:

Europe: weighs just ninety-eight pounds and is designed to be sailed by one person; only women compete in this class, which was introduced at the 1992 Games.

Finn: a 14'6" boat sailed by a single crew member; it is a single sail boat.

Flying Dutchman: a fast, 15'6" boat sailed by two crew members who strap themselves into a harness called a trapeze, so they can lean far out of one side of the boat to balance the sails.

470: a 15'6" boat which has two sails and is sailed by a crew of two.

Windglider (sailboard): a 12'9" surfboard with a sail attached to it; the sailer stands on board like a surfer.

Soling: the largest Olympic boat—26'9" in length and weighing more than a ton; it is raced by a three-person crew.

Star: a 22'7" boat which requires a crew of two.

Tornado: a 20' catamaran (two hulls) sailed by two people.

Yachts are raced in the ocean. The boats navigate over a specific course which is set according to the weather, wind, and tide conditions. The course is defined by floating marks which the yachts must navigate around. In yachting, the lower the point total, the better. Each yacht races seven times, with the best six finishes counting for points.

Summer Games on Water
(continued)

Yachting Activities

1. Do you know the parts of a yacht? Using reference materials, learn about the parts listed below and then write the name of the part on the appropriate line on the yacht.

mainsail	spinnaker	mast
bow	cockpit	hull
rudder	boom	stern

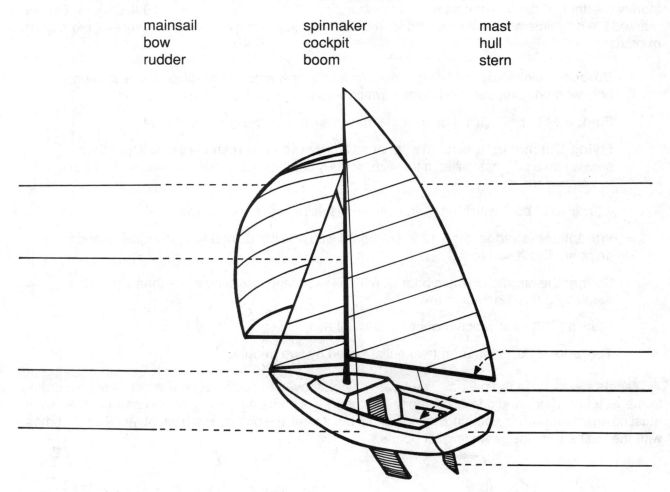

2. The America's Cup is the most famous yacht race. It began in 1851 in the waters off Newport, Rhode Island. Using reference materials, find out what was unique about the America's Cup from 1851 to 1983, what was unusual about the boat used in the 1988 race, and what the big change was in the 1995 race.

_____

_____

_____

_____

Name _____

Gymnastics

Gymnastics was practiced by the ancient Greeks and Egyptians as a means of perfecting the body. Gymnastics is derived from the Greek word *gymnos* meaning "naked." Gymnastic exercises were performed in the nude as a means of preparing young men for battle. Modern gymnastics had its beginning in Germany during the eighteenth century. Young people were encouraged to climb poles, ropes, and ladders, and to balance on beams. Toward the end of the nineteenth century, gymnastic clubs became popular in Europe.

Gymnastics has been a part of the Olympics since the first modern games, when seventy-five athletes from five countries competed. Women were allowed to compete in individual events at the 1952 Helsinki Games. Gymnastics is divided into two categories: artistic gymnastics performed on an apparatus, and rhythmic gymnastics performed with an apparatus. Rhythmic gymnastics was added in 1984 and is open to women only. Gymnasts perform ballet and gymnastic movements to music using ribbons, hoops, and ropes.

Activity

Here are some words that you might hear at a gymnastics meet. Match each word with its definition.

a. dismount   e. tuck
b. layout position   f. release
c. pike position   g. aerial
d. salto   h. stick the landing

_____ a flip or somersault

_____ the body is bent forward more than ninety degrees and the legs are kept straight

_____ a position in which the knees are drawn up to the chest

_____ to land on feet and stand still without stepping or falling

_____ to turn completely over in the air without touching the apparatus

_____ to let go of a bar to perform a move before regrasping the bar

_____ to leave an apparatus at the end of a routine

_____ a position where the body is perfectly straight

Name _____

Gymnastics
(continued)

Women's Events

Vault: an event in which women vault over the width of the vault after sprinting down an 82-foot runway and jumping off a springboard. It enables the gymnast to launch herself into the air. She momentarily places her hands on the horse and pushes off before vaulting over it.

Uneven Bars: an event where the gymnast performs movements using two bars at different heights in a routine that usually lasts less than thirty seconds. The gymnast swings around one bar at a time, but she must switch quickly back and forth between them.

Balance Beam: an event where the athlete must perform many difficult moves on a beam sixteen feet long, four inches wide, and four feet high. Olympic level gymnasts perform somersaults, leaps, handsprings, and tumbling passes on the beam.

Floor Exercise: an event that combines gymnastic and dance elements on a 40-foot square mat. Each routine is performed to music and uses the entire floor space.

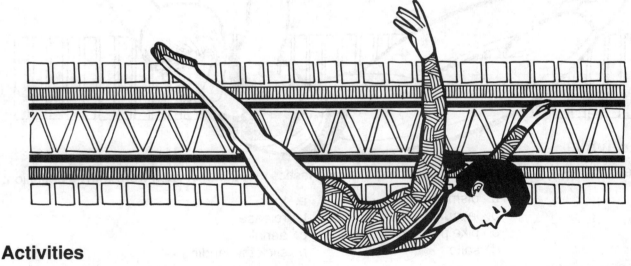

Activities

1. If you were participating in a woman's gymnastic meet, which event do you think would be the most difficult for you? Explain the reasons for your choice.

2. Pretend that you are on the International Olympic Committee to decide on a fifth event for women gymnasts which uses a new apparatus. Name the new event, explain the rules and scoring, and draw the apparatus.

3. Read about three famous women gymnasts: Nadia Comaneci, Olga Korbut, and Mary Lou Retton. Make a report on one of them. Include some information about their training program, the country they represented, the medals they won, and the reasons why they are so important to the world of gymnastics.

Name _____

Gymnastics
(continued)

Men's Events

Floor Exercise: Gymnasts compete on a 40-foot square mat by performing tumbling exercises. They do not perform to music and are not expected to dance.

Pommel Horse (Sidehorse): In this event, the gymnast grabs two wooden handles called pommels and then swings his legs in circles around the sides and top of the horse without stopping or touching the horse.

Still Rings: In this event, the athlete grabs two hanging rings and tries to keep them motionless while performing various movements like circular swings and handstands.

Vault: After taking a running start and jumping off a springboard, the gymnast vaults over the length of the horse. The gymnast pushes off the horse and performs several gymnastic movements in the air.

Parallel Bars: The gymnast performs on two wooden bars and uses arm power to support himself while performing twists, swings, handstands, and flips.

Horizontal Bar: In this event, the gymnast holds one bar with one or both hands and swings many times around it without stopping. He also changes grip, reverses directions, and releases and regrasps the bar.

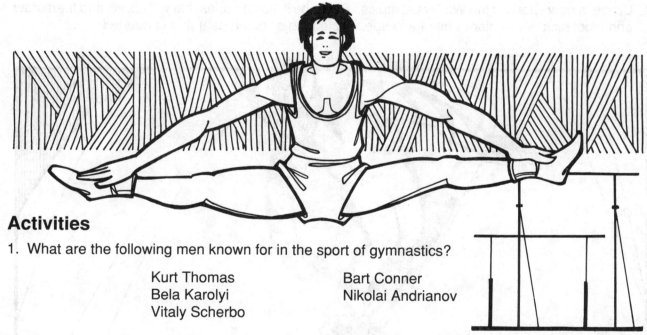

Activities

1. What are the following men known for in the sport of gymnastics?

   Kurt Thomas   Bart Conner
   Bela Karolyi   Nikolai Andrianov
   Vitaly Scherbo

2. Would you be willing to begin a strict training program at an early age so that you could become an Olympic champion? What would you have to give up? Would it be worth it if you won a medal? What if you didn't win? Discuss these questions with your classmates. Take a survey of your classmates to find out how many would want to become an Olympic contender.

Name _____

The Winter Olympics

Many of the skills demonstrated in the Winter Olympics are very old. They developed out of a need to get from one place to another in the ice and snow of cold winter climates. In the Scandinavian countries, skis 5,000 years old have been found. In Scotland, people were skating on ice skates made of iron by 1572, but they had used skates made of wood and bone long before that.

Although there were formal competitions in winter sports in the 1800s, they were not included in the Olympics until 1908, when figure skating was added to the London summer games. In 1920 in Antwerp, Belgium, both ice hockey and figure skating were included as summer events.

When the French were awarded the 1924 Olympics in Paris, they decided to hold an International Winter Sports Week the same year in Chamonix. Members of the International Olympic Committee liked the idea and voted to call this week the Winter Olympic Games. These games were so successful that, with the exception of the war years, the Winter Olympics have been held every four years since.

Activities

1. Write a story or myth about the first person who used skis. Where did he or she get the idea? How were they made?

2. Create a plan for the Winter "Animalympics." List and describe the events. Consider the specific natural abilities of different animals. Then, tell which ones will participate in each event. Choose one event and write a news report or a television commentary about the participants and the actual competition.

3. Create a new sport for the Winter Olympics. Describe it, list the rules that will apply, and then draw and label pictures or diagrams of any special clothing or equipment that is needed.

Name _____

The Winter Olympics
(continued)

The Winter Olympics are held in late January or February. They follow the same traditions as the summer games with parades, ceremonies, medals, and the continuous burning of the Olympic flame.

Many of the nations that participate in the Summer Olympics do not have enough cold weather for their athletes to become accomplished at winter sports. For this reason, fewer nations are able to participate in the winter games. At the Albertville Olympics held in the winter of 1992, there were 64 countries that participated, compared to 172 countries that participated in Barcelona in the summer of 1992.

In 1994, Summer Games and Winter Games were scheduled for the first time in a staggered, four-year cycle (two years apart). For example, Winter Games are scheduled for 2002, 2006, and 2010. Summer Games will take place in 2000, 2004, and 2008.

Winter Olympic Sites

1924	Chamonix, France
1928	St. Moritz, Switzerland
1932	Lake Placid, New York, U.S.A.
1936	Garmisch-Partenkirchen, Germany
1948	St. Moritz, Switzerland
1952	Oslo, Norway
1956	Cortina d'Ampezzo, Italy
1960	Squaw Valley, California, U.S.A.
1964	Innsbruck, Austria
1968	Grenoble, France
1972	Sapporo, Japan
1976	Innsbruck, Austria
1980	Lake Placid, New York, U.S.A.
1984	Sarajevo, Yugoslavia
1988	Calgary, Canada
1992	Albertville, France
1994	Lillehammer, Norway
1998	Nagano, Japan
2002	Salt Lake City, Utah, U.S.A.

Activity

Locate the Winter Olympic sites on a world map. Choose four new locations that would be good choices for future winter games and tell why you chose them.

Winter Olympic Events

Nordic Skiing

Men
10-, 15-, 30-, and 50-kilometer cross-country races
4 x 10-kilometer cross-country relay
70- and 90-meter ski jumping
90-meter team ski jumping
combined ski jumping event
10- and 20-kilometer biathlon
4 x 7.5 biathlon relay

Women
5-, 10-, and 15-kilometer cross-country races
20-30 kilometer cross-country race
4 x 5-kilometer cross-country relay
7.5 and 15-kilometer biathlon
3 x 7.5 biathlon relay

Alpine Skiing

Men
downhill, slalom, giant slalom, super giant slalom
combined (downhill and slalom)

Women
downhill, slalom, giant slalom, super giant slalom
combined (downhill and slalom)

Freestyle Skiing

men's moguls
women's moguls
snowboarding (demonstration sport in 1994)

Winter Olympic Events
(continued)

Figure Skating

men's singles
women's singles
pairs
ice dancing

Ice Hockey

Bobsledding

2-man, 4-man

Luge

Men
single seat, two seat

Women
single seat

Speedskating

Men

500-, 1,000-, 1,500-, 5,000-, 10,000-meter long track speedskating
1,000-meter short track speedskating
5-kilometer short track relay

Women

500-, 1,000-, 1,500-, 3,000-, 5,000-meter long track speedskating
500-meter short track speedskating
3-kilometer short track relay

Name _____

Skis and Sleds

Three types of skiing are included as Winter Olympic events: **Nordic skiing, Alpine skiing, and freestyle skiing**. Nordic, or cross-country, skiing originated in the Scandinavian countries as a reliable means of winter travel. Alpine, or downhill, skiing originated in the Alps, a mountain range that separates France from Switzerland, as an enjoyable means of recreation. In Olympic competition, Nordic skiing includes several different events. These events are cross-country races of varying lengths, ski jumping from various heights, an event that combines cross-country racing with ski jumping, and the **biathlon**, which involves both cross-country skiing and rifle sharpshooting. Olympic Alpine skiing competition includes a downhill race and several slalom events, in which skiers race against time over a zig-zag course. They must move smoothly and cleanly around and between flags on poles.

Americans popularized freestyle skiing, or "hot-dogging," in the 1960s and 1970s. Freestyle skiing consists of aerials, ballet, and **moguls**, which are high-speed turns on a heavily moguled slope (a slope covered with snow bumps). Freestyle skiers use shorter skis and longer, stronger poles than alpine skiers. In mogul freestyle, the judges look for form and technique, the difficulty of two acrobatic moves, and speed. Mogul freestyle became an official medal event in the 1992 Olympics.

Name _____

Skis and Sleds
(continued)

The Winter Olympics also includes two types of sledding events. The sled is an ancient mode of transportation. Before the wheel was invented, platforms with runners were used to haul loads on dry ground, as well as on snow and ice. During the 1500s, people also began to use sleds as a form of recreation. They rode them down snow-covered slopes.

The sleds used in the Winter Olympics are the **bobsled** and the **luge** (loozh). A bobsled is made of aluminum and steel and has a small cowl, or hood, in front to reduce wind resistance. Each sled has either two or four seats. Good sleds cost $25,000 or more and are an important factor in a sport where a hundredth of a second can decide a race. Bobsledding, a team sport, was one of the original Winter Olympic events. In this event, crews of two or four ride their sleds over a curving, downhill course in a race against time. This may sound easy, but it is not. Bobsled crew members practice long hours together so that they will be able to shift their weight from one side to the other at exactly the right moment as they enter the curves. A slight error can cause the team to lose valuable time over the course. A more serious error can cause the bobsled to overturn and bring disaster. Although women were the pioneers of this sport, they have never competed in the Olympics.

The second sledding event, **luge tobogganing**, was added to the Winter Olympics in 1964. Luges are small, lightweight racing sleds. They hold one or two drivers, who control the sleds by using their feet and hand ropes. The luge course is similar to a bobsled run except that it is usually shorter, steeper, and built with more curves. Luge drivers once sat upright as they sped down the course, but today they lean back as far as they can to reduce wind resistance and increase speed. The pressure exerted on the body is often up to seven times the force of gravity. Luge has been described as the most dangerous Olympic sport. The sleds careen downhill at speeds of more than 120 kilometers per hour. Luge is the only Olympic sport that is timed in thousandths of a second.

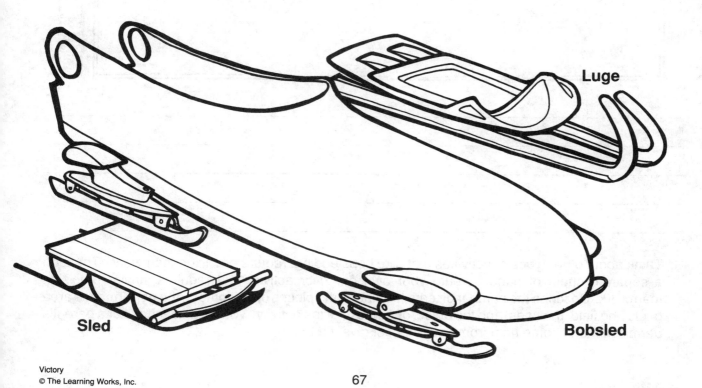

Luge

Sled

Bobsled

Name _____

Skis and Sleds
Activity Sheet

1. Sled speed is affected by three main factors: weight, air resistance, and friction. With this in mind, explain why luge drivers can go faster if they recline rather than sit upright. What other things can a sled team do to make its sled go faster?

2. After looking at a picture of a simple child's sled and at the pictures of the bobsled and the luge that are used in Olympic competition (see page 67), invent a different type of sled either for fun or for competition. In the space provided, draw and label a diagram of your sled. Then, on the lines below, list the ways in which your design is an improvement over previous sled designs.

_____

_____

_____

_____

3. Think about other types of activities that, like bobsledding, require precision teamwork. Then, on a separate sheet of paper, create your own game or activity that requires similar precision teamwork. Describe the number of team members, the pieces of equipment, the performance area or playing field, the rules, and the object or purpose of the activity. With your teacher's or a parent's permission and some help from your friends, give it a try.

Name _____

Frigid Fun

The Winter Olympics are held in a location that is likely to be cold and snowy; however, the weather cannot always be counted on to remain cold, and the skies do not always produce snow when and where it is needed. In 1964, in Innsbruck, Austria, snow did not fall on schedule for the winter games. Fortunately, by working hard, the Austrians were able to preserve most of the snow that had already fallen. They even trucked in snow from other locations.

1. Before the invention of gas or electric refrigerators, people thought of many ingenious ways to preserve winter's ice for use during warmer seasons. Sometimes they kept the ice in holes dug in the sides of hills or packed it in sawdust in specially built icehouses with very thick walls. Why might these methods be effective ways to preserve ice?

2. Experiment to discover the best way to preserve an ice cube other than in a refrigerator or freezer. Try different containers, different packing materials, and different storage areas. Keep a written record of the methods you use and the results you obtain with each method.

3. Hold an Ice Cube Olympics to see who can design the most effective container to preserve an ice cube. You will need to establish some rules. For example, you should limit the size of the containers, make sure that all of the ice cubes are the same size at the beginning of the contest, set a time limit, and decide how the results will be judged and the outcome determined.

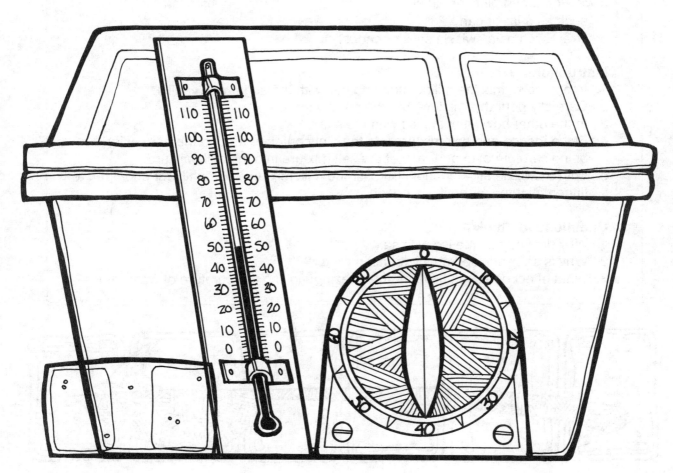

Name _____

More Frigid Fun

1. It is your job to make certain that there is plenty of snow and ice for the Winter Olympics. Although there is snow on the ground now, the weather forecast is for sun accompanied by a warming trend. Brainstorm ways to protect your skiing, skating, and bobsledding areas.

2. Rube Goldberg was an American cartoonist who was known for creating bizarre, elaborate machines that complicated simple, everyday tasks. Design a Rube Goldberg-style snow-making machine. Draw a cartoon of your contraption, and add labels to show how it works.

3. Make your own Vanilla Victory ice cream. Use the recipe below.

❄ Vanilla Victory Ice Cream ❄

Equipment
two small mixing bowls
a spoon
a narrow glass jar, such as an
　　empty spice container
a wide-mouthed pint container,
　　such as a jar or can
a stirrer, such as a swizzle stick or chopstick

Ingredients
$\frac{1}{3}$ cup of milk or half and half
$1\frac{1}{2}$ teaspoons of sugar
2 drops of vanilla
3 cups of crushed ice
3 teaspoons of salt

Instructions
1. In one bowl, mix the milk or half and half with the sugar and vanilla.
2. Carefully pour this mixture into the narrow jar.
3. In the other bowl, mix the ice with the salt.
4. Place the ice-and-salt mixture into the pint container around the narrow jar, being careful *not* to pour any of the salt mixture into the milk mixture.
5. With a swizzle stick or chopstick, stir the milk mixture constantly for about ten to fifteen minutes, or until it is frozen.

Questions to Think About
1. Why did you mix the ice with salt?
2. Why is salt sprinkled on icy roads in winter?
3. What effect does salt have on the freezing/melting temperature of water or ice?

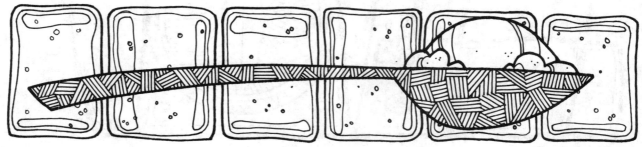

Name _____

Speed on Skates

Speedskating has a history that is longer than that of any other ice sport. More than 500 years ago, a form of speedskating became popular in the Netherlands when people raced down frozen canals. The first recorded speedskating competition took place in England in 1763. In 1850, the introduction of all-steel blades dramatically improved the sport. Unlike the bone, wood, and iron blades of before, the steel blades were light, strong, and maintained their sharp edge for months.

In Olympic **long track speedskating**, two skaters at a time race head-to-head against the clock. The skater with the fastest time at the end of the day is declared the winner. The **short track speedskating** event features "pack" races, with four to six skaters competing at the same time. In this race, time doesn't determine the winner—the first one across the finish line, wins.

Bonnie Blair

Bonnie Blair was taught to skate almost as soon as she could walk. At age fifteen, she realized that she loved speedskating and was very talented at it. She began to train seriously. Now Bonnie Blair is considered the fastest American woman speedskater, and has set American, world, and Olympic records. At Lillehammer, after winning the 500-meter race, Bonnie became the first American athlete to win a gold medal in the same event in three consecutive Olympic Games. She was also the gold medal winner for the 1,000-meter race at both the Albertville and Lillehammer Olympics. Bonnie has won other awards as well. In 1992, she was presented with the Sullivan Award for the nation's top amateur athlete; the United States Olympic Committee Woman Athlete of the Year award; and the Oscar, given by the Norwegians, to the best speedskater in the world. Eric Heiden is the only other American to have received a Norwegian Oscar.

Name _____

Speed on Skates
(continued)

Dan Jansen

Dan Jansen was a gold medal contender when he went into the 1988 Olympics in Calgary. He was expected to win the 500- and 1,000- meter races. Three hours before the 500-meter race, his sister died of leukemia. Suffering from grief, he fell in that race and then fell again four days later just 180 meters from a probable gold medal. He was later awarded the Olympic Spirit Award. With the support of his coach and family, Dan continued to train hard for the 1992 Olympics, but, again, an Olympic medal eluded him. Instead of giving up, Dan stuck with his training program. This time his focus was on the 1994 Olympics in Lillehammer. As Dan sped toward the finish line in the 1,000-meter race, the spectators started cheering—they realized that Dan had a chance to win this race. The cheers grew even louder when the official results were in—Dan Jansen had finally won a gold medal in the Olympic Games.

Activity

1. Speedskating is the fastest an individual can move under his or her own power. Speedskaters can fly around the track at nearly forty miles per hour. Compare that speed with the speed of some of the world's fastest animals.

2. Equipment is important to speedskating. Skintight speedskating uniforms are designed to minimize wind resistance and speedskates have extra-long blades to allow for a longer glide without loss of speed. What other sports or activities have specially designed uniforms or equipment which improves the competitiveness of the athlete? Choose a school game or sport that uses a piece of equipment and, on a separate piece of paper, draw a picture of the object illustrating the changes that you would make that would improve your playing ability.

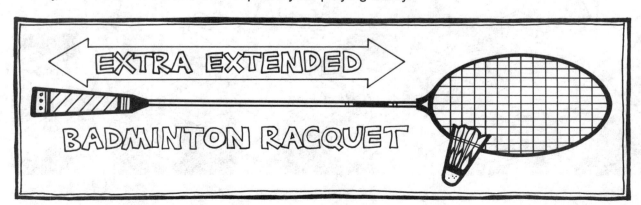

Name _____

Make Your Picks Here for the Summer Olympics

   All of the athletes who compete in the Olympics are winners just by being able to participate. But some of the athletes will be superstars and actually bring home a gold medal. By reading about the people who will compete in each event, and comparing their records and pre-Olympic competitions, you will be able to make a prediction as to who might win a medal. Choose four events that you want to focus on; then make a decision as to which athlete you believe will have the best chance of winning each event. Paste a picture, or make your own drawing, of that athlete in the space provided and complete the chart beneath each picture.

Event: _____
Athlete _____
Country: _____
Reasons for pick: _____
_____

Event: _____
Athlete _____
Country: _____
Reasons for pick: _____
_____

Event: _____
Athlete _____
Country: _____
Reasons for pick: _____
_____

Event: _____
Athlete _____
Country: _____
Reasons for pick: _____
_____

Name _____

Make Your Picks Here for the Winter Olympics

Event: _____
Athlete _____
Country: _____
Reasons for pick: _____
_____

Event: _____
Athlete _____
Country: _____
Reasons for pick: _____
_____

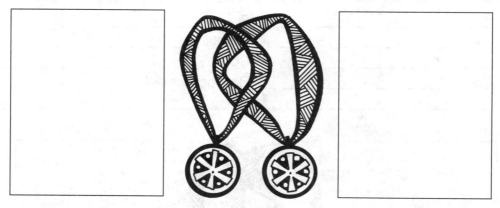

Event: _____
Athlete _____
Country: _____
Reasons for pick: _____
_____

Event: _____
Athlete _____
Country: _____
Reasons for pick: _____
_____

Name _____

The Ideals of the Olympic Games

"The most important thing in the Olympic Games is not to win but to take part, just as the most important thing in life is not the triumph but the struggle." These words were spoken in 1894 by Baron Pierre de Coubertin, founder of the modern Olympic Games. Today, however, it seems that the philosophy of the Olympic Creed is lost with all the attention that is given to gold medal winners.

Is winning everything? Not according to many of the athletes who are examples of amazing courage and dedication. They would probably agree that taking part in the Olympics, and the honor to compete for one's country, were more important than winning.

- Jim Martinson, once a downhill racer who dreamed of going to the Olympics, lost both of his legs in a land mine explosion in Vietnam. Jim never lost sight of his Olympic dream. He competed in the wheelchair race, an event offered for the first time in 1984.

- Paul Hoffman, the only weight lifter from Swaziland at the 1984 Olympics, came in last in all weight lifting divisions. But he had made history as the first and only weight lifter from Swaziland. When asked about his last place, Paul said, "Just to be here to compete, I will remember to my dying day."

- Ed Burke, a hammer thrower, finished seventh in the 1964 Olympics and 12th in the 1968 Games. Eleven years later, after explaining his sport to his young daughters, he made a decision to return to the Olympics. It took until 1984, twenty years after his first Olympics, to make the Olympic team. Although he didn't advance past the qualifying round, he said, "It was a thrill just to walk into the stadium and see so many people and to hear so much cheering. I showed them it's possible to feel satisfaction in just competing, not in the winning."

Name _____

The Ideals of the Olympic Games
(continued)

- In the 1984 Olympics in Los Angeles, Zeina Mina of Lebanon finished 28th in the 400-meter race—dead last. Zeina was her country's leading heptathlete, but she wasn't able to train for her specialty, because bombs prevented her from reaching the stadium in Beirut. Instead, she ran races on the beach, in the subway, and around her neighborhood. For a year she didn't run on a track. Zeina was not concerned about winning. Winning for her was just being able to compete.

- Gabriela Andersen-Scheiss, a Swiss marathon runner, had seen thirty runners pass her during her competition in the 1984 games. Near the finish line, it was clear that the 26-mile race had exhausted her. Medical officers offered to help, but Gabriela waved them off, determined to finish the race. When she finally crossed the finish line, she placed 37th. Gabriela quickly recovered and continues to be an example for many that taking part in a race is more important than winning it.

Activities

1. In your own words, tell what you think "good sportsmanship" means. Has there been a time when you wished you had won a game or contest, but you had to be a good sport about losing? Describe your thoughts in a short story about the incident.

2. Some of the people in the stories above displayed courage. Think of at least five synonyms for "courage." Then use these synonyms in a poem or essay on sports.

3. When asked how he became a hero, John Fitzgerald Kennedy responded, "It was involuntary. They sank my boat." In President Kennedy's book *Profiles in Courage*, he writes, "A man does what he must—in spite of personal consequences, in spite of obstacles and dangers and pressures—and that is the basis of all human morality." Of the men and women Olympic stars that you know about, which ones do you think Kennedy would have considered heroes? Tell why.

Name _____

Olympic Score Sheet

Whether you are attending the Olympic Games in person or watching them on television, you can use this score sheet to keep track of the winners in your favorite events.

Event	Winner	Country	Distance, Time, or Score
	1st		
	2nd		
	3rd		
	1st		
	2nd		
	3rd		
	1st		
	2nd		
	3rd		
	1st		
	2nd		
	3rd		
	1st		
	2nd		
	3rd		
	1st		
	2nd		
	3rd		
	1st		
	2nd		
	3rd		
	1st		
	2nd		
	3rd		

Name _____

Let's Go on an Olympic Scavenger Hunt

How many of the pictures below, which are items associated with an Olympic event, can you identify? Use the information from this book, the sports section of your library, and the resources listed on page 47. Write the name of each object on the line provided, and then identify the sport with which it is used.

Item: _____
Sport: _____
1

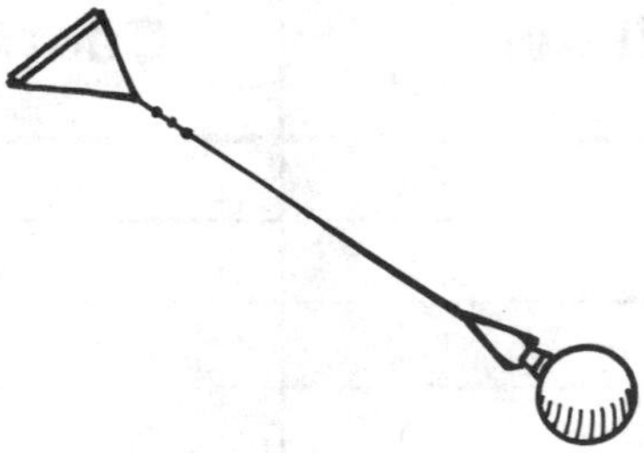

Item: _____
Sport: _____
2

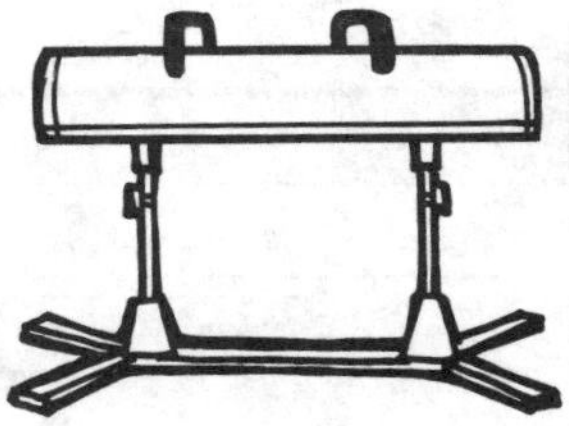

Item: _____
Sport: _____
3

Item: _____
Sport: _____
4

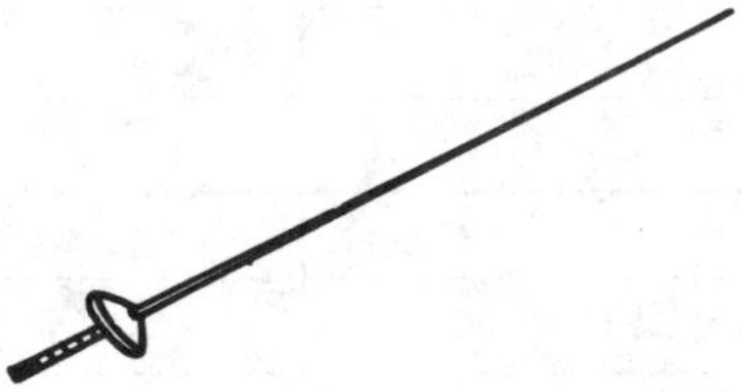

Item: _____
Sport: _____
5

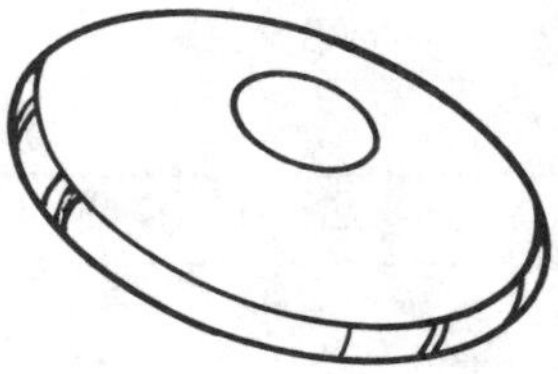

Item: _____
Sport: _____
6

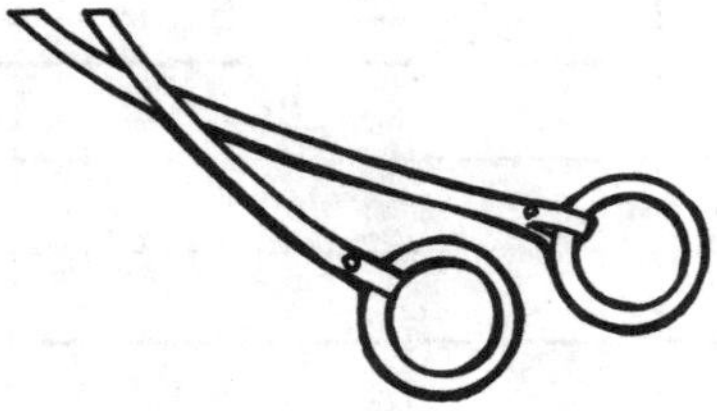

Item: _____
Sport: _____
7

Item: _____
Sport: _____
8

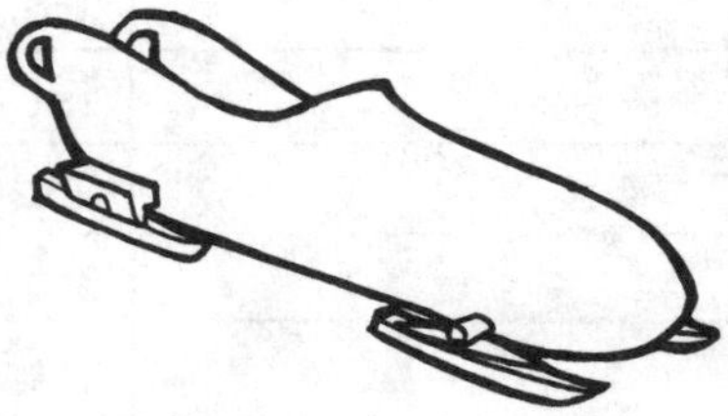

Item: _____
Sport: _____
9

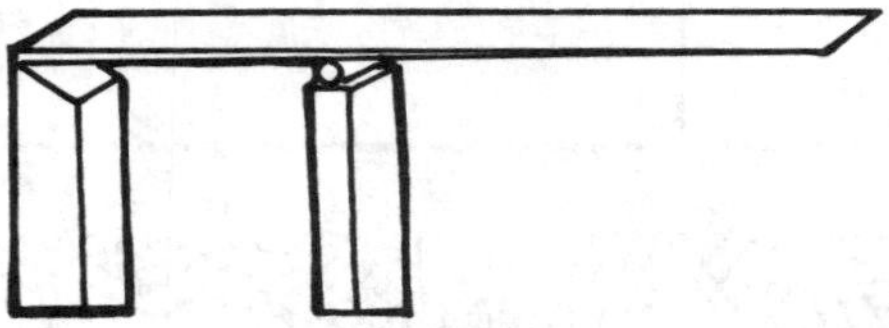

Item: _____
Sport: _____
10

Item: _____
Sport: _____
11

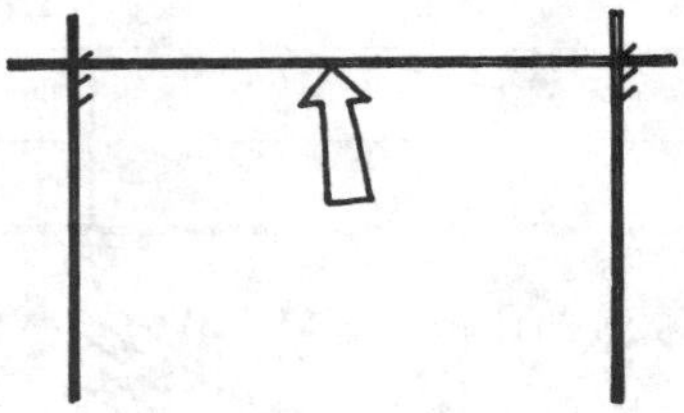

Item: _____
Sport: _____
12

Answer Key

Page 11, It's Greek to Me

a = z	e = r	i = j	m = b	q = g	u = o
b = x	f = p	j = h	n = a	r = i	v = q
c = v	g = n	k = f	o = c	s = k	w = s
d = t	h = l	l = d	p = e	t = m	x = u
y = w	z = y				

Message: The most important thing in the Olympic Games is not to win but to take part.

Page 17, Olympic Pageantry

Activity 2. French = *les Etats-Unis*
Italian = *Stati Uniti*

Page 18, Victorious Vocabulary

1. G   2. A   3. L   4. K   5. B   6. E   7. I   8. N
9. J   10. F   11. D   12. C   13. H   14. M

Pages 20-21, Olympic Myths

The Twelve Olympians: Aphrodite, Apollo, Ares, Artemis, Athena, Hebe, Hephaestus, Hera, Hermes, Hestia, Poseidon, and Zeus. Other deities sometimes included in this group are Demeter, Dionysus, and Hercules.

Page 24, Women Winners

1. B   2. I   3. H   4. I   5. D, F   6. B
7. G   8. H   9. B   10. E, H   11. I   12. J
13. F   14. I   15. F   16. K   17. A   18. C

Page 25, Jackie Joyner-Kersee

1. heptathlon; decathlon; triathlon

Page 27, Mildred "Babe" Didrikson Zaharias

Activity 4. Dressage: the guiding of a horse through various paces and postures without using reins or noticeable signals; Fosbury flop: (track and field) a method of high jumping in which the athlete goes over the bar backwards and head first and lands on his or her back; steeplechase: a horse race over a course having ditches, hedges, and other obstacles (also a cross-country foot race, so named because the runners kept a church steeple in view as their goal.)

Page 32, Oksana Baiul

Activity 1. The Unified Team

Page 35, Compare What They Wear

1. ice hockey   2. track and field   3. soccer
4. swimming   5. Alpine skiing   6. Nordic skiing
7. basketball

Page 37, Amateur—To Be or Not to Be?

Activity 2. An amateur is a person who does something for pleasure, not for money or as a profession. The Latin root of amateur is *amator*, meaning "lover."

Pages 42-47, Olympic Treasure Hunt

1. the twelve most important Greek gods and goddesses
2. on Mount Olympus
3. Answers will vary but may include any six of the following: Aphrodite, Apollo, Ares, Artemis, Athena, Demeter, Dionysus, Hebe, Hephaestus, Hera, Hercules, Hermes, Hestia, Poseidon, and Zeus.
4. Olympia
5. the Olympic Festival *or* the Olympic Games
6. Pelops
7. Oenomaus, King of Pisa
8. Hippodamia
9. Heracles
10. 776 B.C.
11. Coroebus; Elis
12. foot race *or* sprint
13. a crown of olive leaves cut from a sacred olive tree
14. Milo of Croton
15. wrestling
16. by carrying a calf on his shoulders until it was a full-grown bull
17. all-powerful
18. boxing; wrestling
19. He was awarded the victory after he died in the stadium. His opponent raised his hand in defeat without realizing that Arrachion was already dead.
20. Answers will vary but might include archaeological artifacts and ruins; lists kept by historians; monuments, murals, odes written by Greek poets such as Pindar; pictures on Athenian pottery; and words spoken in Greek plays.
21. the Heraea
22. the Greek Goddess, Hera.
23. A.D. 394
24. Emperor Theodosius the Great of Rome
25. The games had lost their religious significance and had degenerated into a carnival. The athletes began demanding money for their performances. Due to widespread corruption, Theodosius stopped the games.
26. Baron Pierre de Coubertin

Answer Key
(continued)

27. in 1896 at Athens, Greece
28. 1,502 years
29. thirteen
30. cycling, fencing, gymnastics, shooting, swimming, tennis, track and field, weight lifting, and wrestling
31. Europe, Asia, Africa, Australia, and America
32. *From left to right:* blue, yellow, black, green, red
33. Swifter, Higher, Stronger
34. Jackie Joyner-Kersee
35. 1992
36. 1900
37. the eighty-meter hurdles and the javelin throw
38. golf
39. Soviet Union
40. Cathy Rigby
41. Nadia Comaneci
42. Patricia McCormick
43. Wilma Rudolph
44. Jim Thorpe
45. Al Oerter
46. Jesse Owens
47. The twelve members of the Dream Team were Magic Johnson, Michael Jordan, Chris Mullin, John Stockton, Patrick Ewing, David Robinson, Charles Barkley, Larry Bird, Karl Malone, Clyde Drexler, Christian Laettner, and Scottie Pippen.
48. the decathlon
49. Mark Spitz
50. Janet Evans

Page 48, Olympic Metrics
1. centimeters
2. meters
3. kilometers
4. longer; $9\frac{1}{3}$ yards
5. slightly longer
6. the 1,500-meter run
7. shorter, $119\frac{1}{2}$ yards
8. 4,500 kilometers
9. 2,823 miles
10. kilometers; 42 kilometers

Page 50, Can You Identify the IOC Abbreviations?
11, 9, 7, 5, 3, 1, 14, 16, 19, 6,
12, 10, 8, 17, 15, 18, 4, 20, 13, 2

Page 56, Summer Games on Water (continued)
Activity 2. Romania, Canada, the United States, and Germany

Page 58, Summer Games on Water (continued)
Activity 1. Column one, top to bottom: spinnaker, mast, bow, hull; column two, top to bottom: mainsail, boom, cockpit, stern, rudder. Activity 2. From 1851 to 1983, the America's Cup was continually in the possession of the U.S. In the 1983 race, however, the U.S. lost the cup to Australia. The boat used by the U.S. in the 1988 race was a multihull craft (catamaran). Although the U.S. won the 1988 race, the Supreme Court ruled that its use of a catamaran posed an unfair advantage and awarded the Cup to New Zealand in 1989. The decision was appealed and subsequently overturned. In the 1995 race, the boat entered by the United States was sailed by an all-woman crew.

Page 59, Gymnastics
d, c, e, h, g, f, a, b

Page 61, Gymnastics (continued)
Activity 1. Kurt Thomas won three U.S. championships in a row (1978, 1979, and 1980). Thomas never competed in the Olympics, however, because of the U.S. boycott of the 1980 Games. Bela Karolyi, a former coach of the U.S. Olympic Team, defected from Romania in 1981. His pupils have included Nadia Comaneci, Mary Lou Retton, and Kim Zmeskal. Vitaly Scherbo, a gymnast for the Unified Team, was awarded a gold medal in 1992 in All-Around competition. Bart Conner took the gold medal in 1984 for his performance on the parallel bars. Nikolai Andrianov participated in the 1972, 1976, and 1980 Olympics, winning more medals than any other male athlete in Olympic history.

Pages 78, Let's Go on an Olympic Scavenger Hunt
1. shuttlecock or bird, badminton; 2. hammer, hammer throw; 3. vaulting horse, gymnastics; 4. scull, rowing; 5. épée, fencing; 6. discus, discus throw; 7. rings, gymnastics; 8. snowboard, freestyle skiing; 9. bobsled, bobsledding; 10. springboard, diving; 11. ice skate, figure skating; 12. crossbar, pole vaulting